扬州园林与住宅

Yangzhou Gardens and Traditional Residences（纪念版）

陈从周
Chen Congzhou

同济大学出版社　上海
TONGJI UNIVERSITY PRESS　SHANGHAI

陈从周先生百年诞辰纪念

Commemorating the Centenary of Chen Congzhou's Birth

2018 年，因中国著名古典园林与建筑艺术家陈从周先生的百年诞辰而非同寻常。

为了这份特别的纪念，我们将陈从周先生的四部经典学术著作《苏州园林》《苏州旧住宅》《扬州园林（与住宅）》《中国名园》汇集再版。文字的重新录入与勘校，照片、测绘图的重新查找与制作……我们倾注满腔心血，将崇敬之情融入每段文字、每张图片的编排与设计之中。

为了明晰文字内容与图片之间的逻辑关系，我们在忠于原书稿素材的基础上，重新调整了图文次序，并对四本书中的照片和测绘图较原版做了局部删减。另外，因新寻找到陈从周先生当年拍摄的扬州园林照片，《扬州园林与住宅》（原《扬州园林》）较原版做了约 50 张图片的增补。

由于汇集再版的四部著作的原版来自不同的年代、不同的英文译者、不同的出版社，因此译文风格与专有名词译法迥异。加之目前园林等专有名词尚未有统一的官方译法（政府部门、景点官网、国际组织、民间等各方的译法不一），作为"纪念版"，为了尽量保持原版的历史风貌与体系完整，对于专有名词的英译，我们只做了所属书内的统一。

四部久负盛名的经典著作，再现一位建筑前辈的魁奇风骨。

———编者按

2018 is a very special year because of the centenary of a great man in the field of Chinese architecture.

To memorize the extraordinary significance, we are going to republish Mr. Chen's four classic academic works: *Suzhou Gardens*, *Traditional Suzhou Residences*, *Yangzhou Gardens (and Traditional Residences)*, and *Famous Chinese Gardens*. We have put great effort into these books, typing and proofreading texts, collecting photos and drawings, editing images... We designed and arranged the layout and pictures with the highest respect for the author.

While trying our best to maintain the authenticity of the contents, we have adjusted the sequence of the contents and deleted some photos and drawings compared to the original, so as to better clarify the relationship between texts and pictures. In addition, due to the newly discovered photos of Yangzhou gardens taken by the author, about 50 pictures in *Yangzhou Gardens and Traditional Residences* (originally *Yangzhou Gardens* ) were added.

Since the original editions of the four reprinted works are from different time, translated by different translators into English, and published by different publishers, the translation styles are not alike, and the proper nouns are translated in different ways. Currently, there is no unified official translation for the proper nouns. For example, for gardens, government departments, official websites of the scene spots, international organizations, and the general public have their own English translations. As the four books published this time are "Centenary Edition", the original historical features and complete system of which should be maintained as much as possible, we have only made the translations of proper nouns consistent within each book.

The four classic works on classical Chinese gardens and residences are revived, reflecting the distinguished character of a trailblazing Chinese architectural master.

— The Editors

# 目录 | Table of Contents

扬州是我国历史上著名的城市，位于长江下游北岸，江淮平原之上，论地理是极其冲要与富庶的地方，地势平坦，气候温和，雨量适中，在7世纪初（隋炀帝）时开凿了大运河，则又使扬州成为南北交通的枢纽，为以后的经济繁荣、技术进步提供了有利条件。现在保留下来的扬州传统建筑兼有南北两地之长，形成了扬州传统建筑的独特风格。

1961年夏，我校建筑系建筑学专业的同学测绘了扬州传统园林与住宅30余处，现汇编成册，作为建筑设计与教学上的参考。

建筑测绘是建筑学专业三年级的教学实习内容，通过测绘增强同学对中国传统建筑的平面布局、空间组合、建筑造型以及色彩、结构、构造与细部等特点的感性认识，掌握测绘方法，提高制图能力，并结合测绘初步了解调查与收集资料的方法。

我国是一个幅员广大、历史悠久的国家。在祖国各地有着丰富多彩的民居，它们是我国古代劳动人民留给我们的优厚遗产。对这份浩如烟海的民居进行调查研究，是一项长期而又艰巨的任务。根据教学单位的情况，结合建筑测绘进行民居调查是一种较

Yangzhou is a historical city located at the north bank of lower Yangtze River and on the Yangtze-Huai Plain. Geographically, Yangzhou is a very important and fertile site with its flat terrain, mild weather and moderate rainfall. In the early seventh century during the Sui Dynasty, Emperor Yang began digging the Grand Canal, which transformed Yangzhou into the transportation junction connecting the South and the North. The Grand Canal provided favorable conditions for economic prosperity and technological advances afterwards. The preserved traditional architecture in Yangzhou has advantages from both the South and the North, forming the unique style of Yangzhou's traditional architecture.

In the summer of 1961, the architecture students from Tongji University surveyed over thirty gardens and residences in Yangzhou. Now the surveying materials are compiled into a book, to serve as a reference for architectural design and education.

As part of third-year students' program of study, they undertake architectural surveys to fulfill their practice requirements. Through surveying, students can strengthen their knowledge of traditional architecture in the aspects of plan layout, spatial combination, and building form, as well as improve their sense of color, structure, tectonics, detail and so on. Students can then master the survey methodology, improve their drawing ability, and also gain the preliminary understanding for research and gathering materials.

China is a large country with a long history and various people living in all parts of the country. Their residences are the generous heritage from the laboring people among our ancestors. It is a long lasting and challenging task to survey and research all these residences. Based on the condition of the university, it may be suitable to conduct the residential research with architectural survey, which is also a relatively good method to combine teaching and research. Throughout the years, we have been to Suzhou, Yangzhou, Songjiang, Qingpu, Wuxi and several other places for residential research and architectural survey. Not only do we complete teaching requirements, but also accumulate research results.

Professor Chen Congzhou was in charge of choosing the survey locations for *Yangzhou Gardens and Traditional Residences*. Students were under the instruction of professor Chen Congzhou, Wu Yiqing, Zheng Xiaocheng, Guan Tianrui, Lu Jiwei and other professors. Professor Chen wrote the essays. Photos were all taken by Professor Chen, except some old ones. Illustrations were rendered by Professor Lu Jiwei. Students who participated in the survey were third year architecture students in the 1961 academic year. Mistakes and flaws are unavoidable based on the students' and professors' abilities. Please advise us of any corrections or suggestions.

Teaching and Research Office of Architectural History

Department of Architecture, Tongji University

July, 1964

为合适的方法，同时也是教学与科研相结合的较好方法。几年来，我们先后进行了苏州、扬州、松江、青浦、无锡等地的民居测绘与调查工作。事实证明，这样不但能够顺利完成教学任务，而且又积累了科学研究成果。

《扬州园林与住宅》测绘对象的确立由陈从周先生负责；测绘工作是在陈从周、吴一清、郑肖成、关天瑞、卢济威等先生指导下进行的；本书文字由陈从周先生执笔；书中照片除若干旧写外，均由陈从周先生拍摄；插图由卢济威先生绘制。参加测绘工作的人员为1961学年建筑学三年级学生。限于师生水平，差错之处在所难免，请读者指正。

同济大学建筑系建筑历史教研室

1964 年 7 月

扬州是一个历史悠久的古城，很早以前就多次出现繁华景象，成为我国经济最为富裕的地方。物质基础的丰厚为扬州文化艺术的发展创造了有利的条件，表现在园林与住宅方面就是其独特的成就和风格。试从历史的发展来看，公元前486年（周敬王三十四年），吴王夫差在扬州筑邗城，并开凿河道，东北通射阳湖，西北至末口入淮，用以运粮。这是扬州建城的开始和"邗沟"得名的由来。扬州由于地处江淮要冲，自东汉后便成为我国东南地区的政治军事重地之一。从经济条件来说，鱼、盐、工、农等各种生产事业都很发达，同时又是全国粮食、盐、铁等的主要集散地之一，而隋唐以后更是我国对外文化联络和对外贸易的主要港埠。这些都奠定了扬州趋向繁荣的物质基础。

Yangzhou, a historically important site in the Jiangsu province, has been one of the most affluent cities in China. From early on, Yangzhou underwent several economic booms and the rich material base provides great opportunities for its development in art and culture. In particular, Yangzhou's landscape and residential architecture established a unique style and achieved several accomplishments. In 486 BC, the 34th year of the reign of King Jing of Zhou, Fuchai, the king of Wu State, began building the city of Hancheng. As part of his efforts, he dug waterways in order to transport grain. The waterways were connected to Sheyang Lake on the northeast direction and connected to Huai River at Mokou on the northwest direction. This marked the beginning of the city of Yangzhou and the name of the canal Hangou. Situated at an important location between the Yangtze River and the Huai River, Yangzhou became a place of political and military importance after the Eastern Han Dynasty (25-220). Economically, fishing, salt making, industrial and agricultural industries all developed well in Yangzhou to make the city as China's major distribution center for grain, salt, iron and so on. Furthermore, after the Sui (281-618) and Tang Dynasties (618-907), Yangzhou became the major port for foreign cultural relations and foreign trade. All these made up the material foundation for its prosperity.

By the Sui-Tang period, Yangzhou had become a place of great importance and wealth.

After Emperor Wen (Yang Jian) founded the Sui
Dynasty by reuniting northern and southern China,
the Yangtze-Huai basin turned into a source of
wealth. Yangzhou, situated in the center of the
area, naturally became prosperous. Later on,
Emperor Yang (Yang Guang) of the Sui came
to Yangzhou, spending recklessly wealth and
proposing large-scale construction for his pleasure
palace. Yangzhou demonstrated unprecedented
prosperity even though its wealth was not carried
on substantially. The canal dug during Emperor
Yang's reign turned Yangzhou into the waterway
hub connecting north and south China, providing
favorable conditions for a later economic
boom. In terms of architectural technology,
northern craftsmen dispatched by the ruling
class interchanged ideas and collaborated with
the craftsmen from regions south of the Yangtze
River; together, they greatly advanced Yangzhou's
architectural development. Poet Du Mu of the Tang
Dynasty wrote in his poem admiring Yangzhou's
flourishing scene, "Who knows while West
Bamboo Road is quiet, Yangzhou is full of singing
and music."

As early as the Northern and Southern
Dynasties (420-589), Xu Zhanzhi from the
territory of the Liu Song Dynasty (420-479) built
Fengting (Wind Pavilion), Yueguan (Moon Tower),
Chuitai (Flute Terrace), Qinshi (Lyre Chamber)
and so on, which were located lower than Pingshan
(Even with Mountain) Hall. During the Zhenguan
era (627-649) of the Tang Dynasty, Pei Chen's

　　隋唐时代的扬州是极其重要而富
庶的地方。从隋文帝（杨坚）统一南
北以后，江淮的富源得到了繁荣的机
会，扬州位于江淮的中心，自然也就
很快地兴盛起来。其后，隋炀帝（杨
广）来到扬州恣意寻欢作乐，并大兴
土木，建造离宫别馆。虽然这时的扬
州开始呈现了空前的繁荣，却不能使
扬州的富庶得到真正的发展。隋炀帝
时，所开凿的运河使扬州成为掌握南
北水路交通的枢纽，为以后的经济繁
荣提供了有利的条件。在建筑技术上，
由于统治阶级派遣来的北方匠师与江
南原有的匠师在技术上进行了交流与
融合，大大地推进了日后扬州建筑的
发展。唐朝诗人杜牧曾用"谁知竹西
路，歌吹是扬州"的诗句来歌咏扬州
当时的繁荣。

早在南北朝时期（420—589），宋人徐湛之在平山堂下建有风亭、月观、吹台、琴室等。到唐朝贞观年间（627—649），裴谌的樱桃园已具有"楼台重复、花木鲜秀"的境界，而郝氏园还要超过它，但这些在唐末都受到了破坏。宋时有郡圃、丽芳园、壶春园、万花园等，多水木之胜。金军南下，扬州受到较大的破坏。正如南宋姜夔于淳熙三年（1176）《扬州慢》词所诵："自胡马窥江去后，废池乔木，犹厌言兵。渐黄昏，清角吹寒，都在空城。"宋金时期，运河已经阻塞。至元初，漕运不得不改换海道，扬州的经济就不如过去繁荣了。元代，仅有平野轩、崔伯亨园等二三例记载。明代初叶，运河经过整修，又成为南北交通的动脉，扬州也重新成了两淮区域盐的集散地；明中叶后，由于资本主义经济的萌芽，城市更趋繁荣，

Yingtao (Cherry) Garden featured "buildings and terraces overlaying, with flowers and plants freshly flourishing," and Hao's Garden had even more complex construction. Unfortunately, both gardens were destroyed at the end of the Tang Dynasty. New gardens emerged during the Song Dynasty (960-1279) with designs emphasizing water and trees, such as Junpu (County Garden), Lifang (Beautiful Flower) Garden, Huchun (Spring In Kettle) Garden, Wanhua (Ten Thousand Flowers) Garden and so on. When the Jurchen troops invaded the south, Yangzhou suffered major destruction. As Jiang Kui of the Southern Song Dynasty (1127-1279) wrote in his poem *Yangzhouman* in 1176, the third year of the Chunxi era, "After barbarian invaders came to the south and left, the city moat and walls of Yangzhou were left destroyed. Locals were fed up with wars and soldiers. As dusk fell, the toneless sound of bugles echoing through the deserted city." At the same time, during the Southern Song Dynasty and the Jin Dynasty (1115-1234), the canal was already blocked. The grain had to be transported by sea by the early Yuan Dynasty (1206-1368), thus Yangzhou's economy was not as prosperous as before. Only several gardens as Pingye (Flat Field) Veranda and Cui Boheng's Garden were recorded. By the early Ming Dynasty (1368-1644), the canal was newly renovated, again transforming into the communicating artery connecting the north and the south. Yangzhou was once more established as the salt distribution center for areas on both sides of the Huai River. After the mid-Ming

Dynasty, capitalist economy emerged and cities prospered again. The salt industry, along with other commerce and handicraft industries, progressed. Yangzhou's economy seemingly reached its pinnacle during the Qing Dynasty (1616-1911) around the seventeenth and eighteenth centuries. Yangzhou's laboring people created unique landscape architecture with their diligence and intelligence. These landscape art works became an important part of China's ancient cultural heritage.

After the mid-Ming Dynasty, merchants in Yangzhou mainly originated from Anhui. Later on, more merchants from Jiangxi, Hunan, Hubei and Guangdong came to Yangzhou to join local merchants in running businesses, making large fortunes. The profits from the business were spent on luxurious lifestyles and large construction of gardens and houses. Anhui merchants brought along Anhui architects and craftsmen, so Anhui's architectural style was absorbed into Yangzhou's architectural style. The convenience of waterway transportation enabled bringing in building materials from various parts of China with ease. Artisans from nearby Xiangshan (in Suzhou) also arrived in boats. Yangzhou's architectural style flourished once more. Garden wise, Meihualing (Plum Flower Ridge), built by prefect Wu Xiu during the Wanli reign (1573-1619), was composed with rockeries as mountains and surrounded by pavilions and terraces. In the late Ming Dynasty, four brothers from the Zheng family each owned a grand garden. These four gardens—Yuanxun's Ying (Shadow) Garden, Xiaru's Xiu (Leisure)

除盐业以外，其他的商业与手工业也都获得了发展。到十七、十八世纪的清代，扬州的经济在表面上可说是到了最繁荣的时期。扬州的劳动人民以他们的勤劳与智慧，创造了独特的园林建筑艺术，为我国古代文化遗产做出了贡献。

明代中叶以后，扬州的商人以徽商居多，其后赣（江西）商、湖广（湖南湖北）商、粤（广东）商等亦接踵而来。他们与本地商人共同经营扬州贸易，所获得的大量资金除了花费在奢侈的生活之外，还花费在大规模地兴建园林和住宅。由于水路交通的便利，随着徽商的到来，又来了徽州的建筑匠师，使徽州的建筑手法融合在扬州建筑艺术之中。各地的建筑材料以及附近香山（苏州香山）的匠师，由于舟运畅通而源源到达扬州，使扬州建筑艺术更为增色。在园林方面，如明万历年间（1573—1619）太守吴秀所筑的"梅花岭"，叠石为山，周以亭台；明末郑氏兄弟（元嗣、元勋、元化、侠如）的"四大园林"——影园（元勋）、休园（侠如）、嘉树园（元嗣）、五亩之园（元化），不论在园的面积上还是造园艺术上都很突出。影园是著名造园家吴江计成的作品，园主郑元勋因受匠师的熏陶亦粗解造园之术。这时的士大夫"寄情"于山水，而匠师们却在地处平原的扬州叠石凿池，以有限的空间构成无限的景色，建造了那"宛自天开"的园林。这些在技术上为后来清乾隆时期（1736—1795）的大规模兴建园林奠定了基础。清兵南下，这些建筑受到了极大的破坏，目前，只有从现存的几处楠木大厅尚能看到当时建筑手法的片段。

　　清初，统治阶级在扬州建有王洗马园、卞园、员园、贺园、冶春园、

Garden, Yuansi's Jiashu (Good Tree) Garden, Yuanhua's Wumu (Five "Mu") Garden—were renowned for their large size and extraordinary landscaping. The owner of Ying Garden, Zheng Yuanxun, acquired his knowledge of gardening from local landscape gardeners and commissioned the celebrated gardener Ji Cheng from Wujiang to design it. Scholar-officials at that time projected their emotions onto mountains and rivers, and the gardeners employed by the officials had to layer rocks and dug ponds on the level ground of Yangzhou. Unlimited spectacles were created in limited spaces, and the gardens were made as if they were built through the divine hand of Mother Nature. This made up the technical foundation for later large-scale construction of landscape architecture during the Qianlong reign (1736-1795) of the Qing Dynasty despite the Manchu invasion and destruction of the south. Nowadays, only a glimpse of the architectural legacies can be seen from the few halls constructed of *Phoebe nanmu* that survived the invasion.

In the early Qing Dynasty, the ruling class built the so-called Eight Famous Gardens in Yangzhou: Wangxianma's Garden (Garden of Librarian Wang), Bian's Garden, Yuan's Garden, He's Garden, Yechun (Going on a Spring Outing) Garden, the South Garden, Zhengyushi's Garden (Garden of Censor Zheng), and Xiao (Slim Bamboo) Garden. During the Qianlong reign, Emperor Gaozong traveled to the south repeatedly for his so-called "inspection tours" which were in fact more for pleasure than for official business.

Specially for his visits, there was a construction spree in which a great number of pavilions, terraces, lofts and gardens were built in Yangzhou to satisfy the emperor's indulgence of pleasure and comfort[1]. Local gentries and merchants also constructed gardens during this time in order to please the royalty, thus acquiring promotions and riches. Hence, from the Slender West lake to Pingshan Hall, "Flowers and willows prosper along both sides of the water banks; buildings and terraces extend all the way till the mountain." The famous scenery was crowned "Twenty-Four Sights." In vol.6 of *Yangzhou Huafang Lu* (*Record of the Painted Pleasure Boats of Yangzhou*), Li Dou quoted Liu Daguan's saying, "Hangzhou exceled with its lakes and mountains. Suzhou was famous for its markets and shops. And Yangzhou was famous for its gardens. These three cities competed each other with their own specialties and no one city surpassed the other two." Qing's ruling class extorted money during the repeated inspection tours to the south under the pretense of colleting "tributes." Merchants first hiked up salt prices and later drew commissions from the so-called "wear and tear" cost. The emperor first deducted a percentage from the sum of salt sales and also manipulated the interest rate on loans granted to the merchants in the name of the state treasury. After a while, the price of "official salt" increased to exorbitant amounts, merchants exploited salt farmers, and locals found it increasingly difficult to afford salt as an essential commodity. Feudal bureaucratic merchants competed to build large

南园、郑御史园、筱园等，号称"八大名园"。乾隆时，因高宗（弘历）屡次"南巡"，为了满足其尽情享乐的欲望，当地大事建筑亭、台、阁、园[1]。扬州的绅商们想争宠于皇室，达到升官发财的目的，也大事修建园林。自瘦西湖至平山堂一带，更是"两堤花柳全依水，一路楼台直到山"。有"二十四景"之称，并著称于世。所以，李斗《扬州画舫录》卷六中引刘大观言："'杭州以湖山胜，苏州以市肆胜，扬州以园林胜，三者鼎胜，不可轩轾。'洵至论也。"清朝的统治阶级正是利用这种"南巡"的机会进行搜刮，美其名为"报效"。商人在盐中"加价"，继而又"加耗"，皇帝从中取利，在盐中提成，名"提引"。皇帝还发官款借给商人，生息取利，称为"帑利"。日久以后，"官盐"价格日高，商人对盐民的剥削日益加重，而广大人民的吃盐也更加困难。封建的官商将剥削得来的资金任意挥霍，争建大型园林与住宅。这时期的园林兴造之风正如《扬州画舫录》谢溶生序文中所说："增假山而作陇，家家住青翠城闉；开止水以为渠，处处是烟波楼阁。"流风所及形成了一种普遍造园的风气。除瘦西湖上的园林外，如天宁寺的行宫御花园、法净寺的东西园、盐运署的题襟馆、湖南会馆的棣园，以及九峰园、乔氏东园、秦氏意园、小玲珑山馆等都很著名。其他如祠堂、书院、会馆，下至餐馆、妓院、浴室等，也都模拟着园林叠石引水，栽花种竹了。这种庭院内略加点缀的风气似乎已成为建筑中不可缺少的部分。

从整个社会来看，乾隆以后，清朝的统治开始动摇，同时中国长期的

gardens and luxurious residences for themselves with their ill-begotten profits. The trend of garden construction swept the whole city of Yangzhou. Xie Rongsheng described the trend in his preface to *Yangzhou Huafang Lu*, "Rockeries were added to make ranges, hence each family lives in an emerald city; resting water is dredged to become canals, everywhere stands mist-covered buildings and lofts." Besides gardens on the Slender West Lake, Yangzhou was filled with many other well-known gardens such as Xinggong Yuhuayuan (Imperial Garden in the Temporary Palace) in Tianning Temple, the East and West Gardens in Fajing Temple, Tijin Guan (Place for Expressing the Mind) in the Salt Shipping Administration, Diyuan Garden in the Provincial Guild Hall of Hunan, as well as Jiufeng (Nine Peaks) Garden, Qiao's East Garden, Qin's Yiyuan Garden, and also Xiaolinglongshan Guan (Small Exquisite Mountain House). Other places such as ancestral halls, academy halls, guild halls and even restaurants, brothels, and bath houses all followed suit to build rockeries, channel in water, and plant flowers and bamboos. The tendency of decorating courtyards had become an indispensable part of architecture.

After the reign of the Qianlong Emperor, the Qing empire became unstable. At the same time, China's two-thousand-year feudalism system was falling apart. Qing's succeeding emperors stopped their repetitive "south inspection tours." Class contradictions and national conflict sharpened in China as the pressures of Western capitalist powers mounted. By the reign of the Jiaqing Emperor, the salt industry monopoly in Yangzhou had declined. After the Opium War, with the signing of the Treaty of Nanking, China was forced to open up five cities as new trade ports: Shanghai, Ningbo, Xiamen, Fuzhou and Guangzhou. Under the completion of the Tianjin-Pukou Railway and the advanced development of marine transportation, Yangzhou lost its leading position in national economy and transportation. In 1834, the fourteenth year of the Daoguang reign, Ruan Yuan wrote "Postscript to *Yangzhou Huafang Lu*" and later, in 1839, the nineteenth year of the Daoguang reign, he wrote the "Second Postscript." In both essays, he described Yangzhou as a barren landscape where "no guests would stay in the deserted loft and no woodsmen would collect the falling trees and woods."[2] Although many records blamed the destructions of the gardens near the Slender West Lake on the Taiping Heavenly Kingdom Uprising army's 1853 invasion of Yangzhou, these words were written 19 years earlier. After the Xianfeng and Tongzhi reigns, Yangzhou was caught between prosperity and downfall. The seeming prosperity was staged by local officials and merchants who made their fortune through quelling the Taiping Heavenly Kingdom Uprising in an attempt to make peace during the decaying Qing empire. During the years of Republic of China, salt merchants lost opportunities to make profits and used up their savings with the abolition of "salt tickets" for trading salt. They dismantled their houses and rockery mountains to sell the raw materials, thus destroying their gardens and large residences.

封建社会也走向下坡，清帝就不再敢"南巡"了。国内的阶级矛盾与民族矛盾正酝酿着大规模的斗争，西方资本主义的浪潮日益紧逼，也动摇了封建社会的基础。到嘉庆时，扬州盐商日渐衰落。鸦片战争后，继以《江宁条约》五口通商，津浦铁路筑成，同时海上交通日趋发达，扬州在经济、交通上便失去了其原有的地位。早在道光十四年（1834），阮元作《扬州画舫录跋》，道光十九年（1839）又作《后跋》，历述他所看见的衰败现象已到了"楼台荒废难留客；林木飘零不禁樵"的地步 [2]，比太平天国军于 1853 年攻克扬州还早 19 年。由此可见，过去的许多记载把瘦西湖一带园林毁坏的责任硬加于农民军身上显然是错误的。咸丰、同治以后，扬州已呈时兴时衰的"回光返照"状态，所谓"繁荣"只是靠镇压太平天国起家的官僚富商在苟延残喘的清朝统治政权的末期粉饰太平而已。民国以后，由于"盐票"的取消，盐商无利可图，坐吃山空，因而都以拆屋售料，拆山售石为生。园林与大型住宅渐趋被破坏之势。

扬州位于我国南北之间，在建筑上有其独特的成就与风格，是研究我国传统建筑的一个重要地区。很明显，扬州的建筑是北方"官式"建筑与江南民间建筑两者之间的一种介体。这与清帝"南巡"、四商杂处、交通畅达等有关，但主要还是匠师技术交流的作用。清道光间钱泳的《履园丛话》卷十二载："造屋之工，当以扬州为第一。如作文之有变换，无雷同，虽数间小筑，必使门窗轩豁，曲折得宜……盖厅堂要整齐，如台阁气象；书斋密室要参错，如园亭布置，兼而

Situated between southern and northern China, Yangzhou's architecture achieved breathtaking accomplishments and developed a unique style, which makes Yangzhou an important area for the study of traditional Chinese architecture. Yangzhou's architecture mediates between northern royal architecture and southern architecture of regions south of the Yangtze River. The mixing of styles is not simply the result of the Qing emperor's "south inspection tours," the gathering of merchants from all over China, and the convenience of transportation, but mainly due to the communication between technicians and craftsmen. Qian Yong of the Daoguang reign wrote in vol.12 of *Lüyuan Conghua (Collected Talks of Lüyuan Garden)*, "Yangzhou stands first in the technology of building construction. Just as texts can be written in various styles, no two buildings stand the same. Even if a building has several rooms, it must have high and wide doors and windows, and the interior space must be thoughtfully intricate...The lobby and main rooms should be square and organized, as austere as official's mansion; the studies and back rooms should be distributed sparsely, like pavilions in a garden. A building is a masterpiece only when it possesses both." Interior decoration in Yangzhou's buildings is no less intricate than building construction. Quoted from the same book above, "Zhou's Principles for interior decoration were only mastered by Yangzhou people. The principles were named after the person surnamed Zhou, who laid down the idea from the late Ming

Dynasty." The important decoration of Beijing's Yuanmingyuan Garden followed after Zhou's Principles, a tribute from Yangzhou[3]. There are other master craftsmen of interior decoration, such as Gu Licheng and Cheng Lie. Yao Weichi, Shi Songqiao, Wen Qi, Xu Lü'an, as well as the Brothers Huang Sheng and Huang Lüxian (also Lühao and Lü'ang), were all specialists of architecture and building furnishing. Moreover, according to vol.2 of *Yangzhou Huafang Lu*, "Yangzhou stands out with its famous gardens, and gardens stand out with stacked rockwork." In Yangzhou, there were a great many masters specializing in stacking rockwork as well. During the Ming and Qing Dynasties, there was Ji Cheng, who stacked the artificial mountain for Ying Garden; Shitao, who created Wanshi (Ten Thousand Rocks) Garden and Pianshi Shanfang (Small Rock Mountain Villa); Zhang Lian, who stacked the rocks for the mountain in Baisha Cuizhu (White Sand and Green Bamboos) and Jiang Cun (Riverside Village); Qiu Haoshi, who built the Xuan-stone (from Xuancheng, Anhui) mountain at Yixing (Pleasing One's Nature) Hall; Taoist Dong, who built Jiushishan (Nine-Lion Mountain); Ge Yuliang, who piled up rocks for Qin's Xiaopangu (Small Meandering Valley); and Wang Tianyu[4], Zhang Guotai and many others. The latecomer builder Yu Jizhi piled up rockery mountains for Cuiyuan Garden, Yilu, Paolu, Weipu, Yechun Garden and so on. Some of these master builders were from Yangzhou, while others originated from elsewhere. They frequently

有之，方称妙手。"在装修方面，也同样考究，据同书卷十二载："周制之法，惟扬州有之。明末有周姓者，始创此法，故名周制。"北京圆明园的重要装修就是采用"周制"手法，由扬州"贡"去的[3]。其他名匠谷丽成、成烈等都精于宫室装修。姚蔚池，史松乔，文起，徐履安，黄晟、黄履暹兄弟（履昊、履昂）等在建筑及园林总体布置方面都有不同的造诣。又据《扬州画舫录》卷二记载："扬州以名园胜，名园以叠石胜。"在叠石方面，名手辈出。明清两代有叠影园山的计成，叠万石园、片石山房的石涛，叠白沙翠竹与江村石壁的张涟，叠怡性堂宣石山的仇好石，叠九狮山的董道士，叠秦氏小盘谷的戈裕良，以及王天于[4]、张国泰等。晚近有叠萃园、怡庐、匏庐、蔚圃和冶春等的余继之。

他们有的是当地人，有的是客居扬州的外地人，在叠山技术方面，互相交流，互相推敲，都各具有独特的造诣，在扬州留下了不少的艺术作品，使我国叠山艺术得到了进一步的提高。

关于扬州园林及建筑的记述，除通志、府志、县志记载外，尚有清乾隆间的《南巡盛典》《江南胜迹》《行宫图说》《名胜园亭图说》，程梦星《扬州名园记》《平山堂小志》，汪应庚《平山堂志》、赵之壁《平山堂图志》、李斗《扬州画舫录》，稍后的阮中《扬州名胜图记》、钱泳《履园丛话》，道光间骆在田《扬州名胜图》，以及晚近王振世《扬州览胜录》、董玉书《芜城怀旧录》等，而尤以《扬州画舫录》记载最为详实，其中《工段营造录》一卷，取材于《大清工部工程做法则

discussed and scrutinized together the craft of rockery mountains. Each of the builders left a unique legacy for Yangzhou, spotlighting the art of rockery mountains.

General histories, prefecture and county records documented gardens and buildings in Yangzhou. More records can be found in books such as *Nanxun Shengdian* (*Grand Ceremony of Southern Inspection Tours*), *Jiangnan Shengji* (*Scenic Sites of the Jiangnan Area*), *Xinggong Tushuo* (*Illustration of Temporary Palaces*), *Mingsheng Yuan-Ting Tushuo* (*Illustration of Gardens and Pavilions*), Cheng Mengxing's *Yangzhou Mingyuan Ji* (*Records of Famous Gardens in Yangzhou*) and *Pingshantang Xiaozhi* (*A Compact Record of Pingshan Hall*), Wang Yinggeng's *Pingshantang Zhi* (*Records of Pingshan Hall*), Zhao Zhibi's *Pingshantang Tuzhi* (*Illustration of Pingshan Hall*) and Li Dou's *Yangzhou Huafang Lu*, all of which are from the Qianlong reign of the Qing Dynasty. Later, works such as Ruan Zhong's *Yangzhou Mingsheng Tuji* (*Illustration of Scenic Spots in Yangzhou*), Qian Yong's *Lüyuan Conghua*, and Luo Zaitian's *Yangzhou Mingsheng Tu* (*Paintings of Scenic Spots in Yangzhou*) appeared during the Daoguang reign. More recent works such as Wang Zhenshi's *Yangzhou Lansheng Lu* (*Records of Scenic Spots in Yangzhou*) and Dong Yushu's *Wucheng Huaijiu Lu* (*Memoir of Wucheng*) also featured such records. Among all the works, *Yangzhou Huafang Lu* provides the most complete and truthful records; in particular, the volume titled *Gongduan Yingzao Lu* (*Notes on Sections of Construction Projects*) is based on *Daqing Gongbu Gongcheng Zuofa Zeli* (*Imperial Specifications for State Buildings from the Qing Dynasty*) and *Yuanmingyuan Zeli* (*Imperial Specifications of Yuanmingyuan Garden*) and utilizes great references and allusions, which preceded all books written before it.

Yangzhou sits on the north side of the lower Yangtze River, facing Zhenjiang across the river. It borders the great river on the south, with Shugang Ridge to the north, Saogou Mountain to the west, and the Grand Canal to the east. Yangzhou's terrain is relatively flat, though higher in the northwest and lower in the southeast. Its soil falls into two broad categories: calcium-rich clay in the hilly area on the northwest, and sandy soil in the southeast alluvial plain, with a layer of rubble above ground. Yangzhou's climate falls into the north temperate zone, in gradual transition to the subtropical zone. Summer's maximum average temperature is around 30 degrees Celsius, and winter's minimum average temperature is around 1 to 2 degrees Celsius. The ocean wind in close proximity makes the temperature cool in the summer and rather cold in the winter. Soil frozen depth is usually around 10 to 15 centimeters, and annual rainfall is normally above 1000 millimeters. The area stands in a seasonal monsoon area, with mostly east wind in summer, and northeast wind in winter. Prevailing wind direction is northeast

例》与《圆明园则例》，旁征博引，有历来谈营造所不及之处。

扬州位于长江下游北岸，与镇江隔江对峙，南濒大江，北负蜀冈，西有扫垢山，东沿运河，就地势而论，较为平坦，西北略高而东南稍低。土壤大体可分两类：西北山丘地区属含钙的黏土；东南为冲积平原，地属砂积土，地面上则多瓦砾层。扬州气候属北温带，为亚热带的渐变地区。夏季最高平均温度在30℃左右，冬季最低平均温度在1℃～2℃。因为离海很近，夏季有海洋风，所以较为凉爽，冬季则略寒冷。土壤冻结深度一般为10～15厘米，年降雨量一般都在1000毫米以上。属季候风区域，夏季多东风，冬季多东北风。常年的主导风向为东北风。在台风季节，还受到一定的台风影响。

扬州既具有平坦的地势、温和的气候、充沛的雨量以及较好的土质，自然环境有利于劳动生产与生活，又地处交通的中心，商业发达，因此历来便成为繁荣的所在，从而促进了建筑的发展。不过在这样的自然条件下，以建筑材料而论，扬州缺乏木材与石料，因此大都是仰给于外地。在官僚富商的住宅与园林中，更出现了珍贵的建筑材料，如楠木、紫檀木、红木、花梨木、银杏木、大理石、高资石、太湖石、灵璧石、宣石等。

当时扬州园林与住宅的分布比较集中在城区，而最大的建筑又多在新城部分。按其发展情况，过去旧城居住者为士大夫与一般市民，而新城则多盐商。清中叶前，盐商多萃集在东关街一带，如小玲珑山馆、寿芝园（个园前身）、百尺梧桐阁、约园与后来的逸圃等，较晚的有地官第的汪氏小

throughout the year, and affected by typhoons to a certain degree during the season.

Yangzhou's natural environment is made up of flat terrain, moderate climate, abundant rainfalls and satisfactory soil quality, which is conducive to labor production and livelihood. As a hub of transportation, and with thriving commerce, Yangzhou has always been a prosperous center, particularly for the development of architecture. However, given its natural condition, Yangzhou lacks architectural materials such as timber and rocks, and thus has to depend on imports. Residences and gardens for government officials and rich merchants had precious materials, such as *Phoebe nanmu*, red sandalwood, mahogany, rosewood, gingko, marble, and stones from Gaozi, Lake Tai in Jiangsu, and from Lingbi and Xuancheng in Anhui.

Most of Yangzhou's gardens and residences were in the downtown and the largest buildings were in the New City. In the past, scholar-officials and ordinary citizens lived mostly in the Old City and salt merchants lived in the New City. Before the mid-Qing Dynasty, salt merchants mostly gathered on Dongguan Street, including Xiaolinglongshan Guan, Shouzhi (Longevity Fungus) Garden (predecessor of Geyuan Garden), Baichi Wutong (Hundred Feet Phoenix Tree) Belvedere, Yueyuan Garden, and later Yipu. Later, there were Wangshi Xiaoyuan (Wang's Small Garden) at Diguandi and the Cangzhou Villa at Ziqidonglai Xiang from the late Qing Dynasty. The cluster of buildings later spread to Huayuan

Xiang and Nanhexia, for example Qiusheng Guan (Autumn Sound Mansion), Suiyue Dushu Lou (Loft for Reading along the Moon), Pianshi Shanfang, Diyuan Garden, Xiaopangu, Jixiao Shanzhuang (Jixiao Villa, also known as the Ho Family Garden or He Garden) and so on. These gardens and residences were fenced by tall walls, and their exteriors looked very similar to those in the cities south of the Yangtze River. Buildings in the Old City were in general lower and smaller, but they lined up nicely in the lanes and alleys, which kept the simple style native to North Suzhou, due to the economic conditions of the local residents. Better residential neighborhoods always sat at the convenient spot for road and waterway transportation, close to the Salt Shipping Administration and the commercial areas.

In Yangzhou, around thirty gardens remain relatively intact today. Classic examples include Pianshi Shanfang, Geyuan Garden, Jixiao Shanzhuang, Xiaopangu, Yipu, Yuyuan Garden, Yilu, Weipu and so on. Compared to gardens, a larger number of residences are well-preserved, for example the residences owned by the families Lu, Wang, Zhao, Wei and others, which are emblematic of various styles.

苑、紫气东来巷的沧州别墅等，亦与此相邻。同时又渐渐扩展到花园巷南河下一带，如秋声馆、随月读书楼、片石山房、棣园、小盘谷、寄啸山庄（又名"何园"）等。这些园林与住宅的四周都筑有高墙，外观多半与江南的城市面貌相似。旧城部分的建筑一般较低小，但坊巷排列却很整齐，还保留了苏北地区朴素的地方风格，这是与居住者的经济基础分不开的。较好的居住区总是在水陆交通便利的区域，接近盐运署和商业地区。

目前，扬州城区还保存得比较完整的园林大小尚有30处，具有典型性的，要推片石山房、个园、寄啸山庄、小盘谷、逸圃、余园、怡庐和蔚圃等。住宅为数尚多，如卢宅、汪宅、赵宅、魏宅等皆为不同类型的代表。

## 片石山房（94—95 页）

片石山房一名"双槐园"，在新城花园巷何芷舠宅内，初系吴家龙的别业，后属吴辉谟[5]。今尚存假山一丘。相传为石涛手笔，被誉为石涛叠山的"人间孤本"。假山南向，从平面看来是一座横长形的倚墙山。西首以今存气势来看，应为主峰，迎风耸翠，奇峭迎人，俯临着水池。人们从飞梁（用一块石造成的桥）经过石磴，有腊梅一株，枝叶扶疏。曲折地沿着石壁可登临峰顶，峰下筑正方形的石室（用砖砌）两间，所谓"片石山房"就是指此石室说的。向东山石蜿蜒，下面筑有石洞，很是幽深，运石浑成，仿佛天然。可惜洞西的假山已倾倒，山上的建筑物也不存在，无法看到它原来的全貌了。这种布局的手法大体上还继承了明代叠山的惯例，不过重点突出，使主峰与山洞都更为显著罢了。全局的主次分明，虽然地形不大，

**Pianshi Shanfang (Page 94-95)**

Also known as Shuanghuai (Twin Pagoda Trees) Garden, Pianshi Shanfang is located inside He Zhidao's residence in the New City's Huayuan Xiang. It was Wu Jialong's villa before Wu Huimo took over[5]. An artificial mountain remains in the garden, said to be Shitao's work. It is renowned as Shitao's only existent rockery mountain bequeathed on humanity. The artificial mountain faces south and has a long, rectangular-shaped layout leaning towards the wall. Judging from today's appearance, the west end seems to be the main peak, standing next to the pond, welcoming visitors with its rare and verdant top, rising up in the wind. When visitors walk across the flying bridge (a bridge made of an entire stone), passing the stone stairway, they come across a winter sweet, which has lush leaves and well-composed branches. Following the path by the cliff, visitors reach the peak. Below the peak there are two square brick rooms. "Pianshi Shanfang" (Small Rock Mountain Villa) is named after these two rooms. As the mountain winds eastward, there is a deep and serene stone cave underneath the mountain, made up of small rocks, integrated together like a work of nature. Unfortunately, due to collapse of the rock works west of the cave and the destruction of buildings on the top of the mountain, we cannot see its complete, original form. This layout inherited the method of large-scale rock piling of the Ming Dynasty. Key points are highlighted, with the main peak and mountain cave emphasized. The whole plan of the garden has a clear hierarchy. Though the site is not huge, it is laid out naturally, with appropriate and sophisticated density and some very outstanding stones of rugged-shapes, truly embodying the name, "Small Rock." Yangzhou's style of artificial mountains is suited to using small rock materials. Shitao once masterfully piled up the mountains for Wanshi Garden, for which he must have used very small rocks to build the mountains. Before he constructed Pianshi Shanfang, he had carefully chosen stones based on their size and the verticality and horizontality of their veins and wrinkles. He grouped the rocks together, mimicking real mountains' shapes, applying painting theory of "using light ink strokes to represent mountain peaks, as if the strokes are coming from the peaks" from his book, *Kugua Heshang Lun Hua Lu* (*Monk Bitter Gourd on Painting*), and the method that he mentioned in the foreword to his painting *Kugua Xiaojing* (*A Small Landscape Painting by Monk Bitter Gourd*), "One peak suddenly ascends, connecting the ridge and breaking the moat. Changes are so sudden and switch between connection and disconnection." Following the theorem, the mountain is tall and the cave is deep, with consistent texturing of veins and wrinkles and without a trace of carving. The overall garden design is concise, with a harmonious balance between fullness and emptiness. According to vol.20 of *Lüyuan Conghua*, "Pianshi Shanfang is located at Huayuan Xiang in Yangzhou's New City. Behind two halls there is a square pond, on which sits a Lake Tai stone mountain. This ingenious and imposing mountain is about 50 to 60 feet high. It is said that the mountain was created by Monk Shitao. The land was part of Wu's residence, and it was later owned by a female matchmaker who converted it into a noodle restaurant and also a theater. The grand hall was remodeled to the same style as the theater outside

布置却很自然，疏密适当，片石峥嵘，很符合"片石山房"的这个名字的含义。扬州叠山以运用小料见长，石涛曾经叠过万石园，想来便是运用高度的技巧，将小石拼镶而成。在堆叠片石山房之前，石涛对石材同样进行了周密的选择，以石块的大小，石纹的横直，分别组合模拟成真山形状。他还采用了其画论上的"峰与皱合，皱自峰生"（见石涛《苦瓜和尚论画录》）的道理，叠成"一峰突起，连冈断堑，变幻顷刻，似续不续"（见石涛《苦瓜小景》题辞）的章法。因此，虽高峰深洞，却一点没有人工斧凿痕迹，显出皱法的统一。全局紧凑，虚实对比有方。按《履园丛话》卷二十："扬州新城花园巷，又有片石山房者。二厅之后，湫以方池，池上有太湖石山子一座，高五六丈，甚奇峭，相传为石涛和尚手笔。其他系吴氏旧宅，后为一媒婆所得，以开面馆，兼为卖戏之所，改造大厅房，仿佛京师前门外戏园式样，俗不可耐。"据以上的记载与志书所记，地址是相符合的，两厅今尚存一座面阔三间的楠木厅，它的建筑年代当在乾隆年间。山旁还存有走马楼（串楼），池虽被填没，可是根据湖石驳岸的范围考寻，尚能想象到旧时水面的情况，假山所用湖石与记载亦能一致。山峰高出园墙，它的高度和书上记载的相若，顶部今已有颓倾。至于叠山之妙，独峰依云，秀映清池，确当得起"奇峭"二字。石壁、磴道、山洞三者最是奇绝。石涛叠山的方法对后世影响很大，而以乾嘉年间的戈裕良最为杰出。戈氏的叠山法，据《履园丛话》卷十二："……只将大小石钩带联络，如造环桥法，可以千年不坏，要如真山洞壑一般，然后方称能事。"苏州的环秀山庄、常熟的燕园与已毁的扬州秦氏意园小盘谷皆出自戈氏之手，前两处都保存了这种"钩带联络"的做法。

Qianmen in the capital. It was terribly tacky." The address mentioned above is the same as in the local gazetteers. Only one out of the two halls remain today—a three-framed hall of *Phoebe nanmu*. It was built during the Qianlong reign of the Qing Dynasty. Beside the artificial mountain, there still stands a "zoumalou" (a storied building compound connected by walkways, spacious enough for horses to trot through, also known as "chuanlou," meaning "stringed storied building"). Though the pond has been filled, the old image of the pond can still be imagined by tracing the Lake Tai stone's embankment. The Lake Tai stones as part of the artificial mountain is also mentioned in the records. The peak towers above the surrounding garden wall and its height are also similar to the description in the book, though the tip is already decayed. The mountain peak stands by the clouds, with its shadow cast in the clear pond. The subtleness of the rockeries is worthy of the description "ingenious and imposing," and the cliff, stone stairway and cave are the three most distinctive of all. Shitao's artificial mountain construction expertise greatly influenced later generations, and Ge Yuliang, a rockery master during the reigns of Qianlong and Jiaqing, was the most significant one who inherited Shitao's knowledge. Ge's craftsmanship is recorded in vol.12 of *Lüyuan Conghua*, "If large and small stones are locked and connected as the construction method for a chain bridge, then the rockery mountain can last for a thousand of years. Moreover, the rockery also has to be as vivid as a real mountain or cave in order for the artificial mountain to be crowned as a masterpiece." Ge Yuliang's mountain works were in Huanxiu Shanzhuang (Mountain Villa with Embracing Beauty) in Suzhou, Yanyuan Garden in

Changshu, and the already destroyed Xiaopangu in Qin's Yiyuan Garden. Today, the first two gardens' artificial mountains still preserve the method of interlocking stones.

### Geyuan Garden (Page 96-115)

Geyuan Garden on Dongguan Street was built by Huang Yingtai (Zhiyun), the chief administrator of the salt industry of Huainan and Huaibei areas during the Jiaqing and Daoguang reigns of the Qing Dynasty. The Garden was named after Yingtai's style name Geyuan, and also for the thousands of bamboos planted in the garden. According to Liu Fenggao's *Geyuan Ji (A Description of Geyuan Garden)*, the garden sits on the former site of the Shouzhi Garden. The original mountain was said to be Shitao's work, though the attribution is disputed. Shitao was considered probably due to the yellow-stone artificial mountain's resemblance to Mount Huangshan in Anhui, whose scenery Shitao was adept at painting. Geyuan Garden used to cover a larger site than today. After the residence was renovated, only the central and eastern sequences of houses remained and the front door and gate house were demolished. The exquisite brick carvings on the screen wall is still well-preserved. Each sequence of houses has three rows of courtyards interconnected. The two columns in the central bay of the hall in the central sequence were removed so that it could also be used as an opera chamber. Every hall is accompanied with a courtyard, which have various styles of parterres. The serene bamboos cast shadows and the flowers are fragrant. The garden is at the back of the residence, and visitors enter through a fire lane (a small lane by the side of the houses). In the garden, there is

## 个园（96—115 页）

个园在东关街，是清嘉庆、道光间盐商两淮商总黄应泰（至筠）所筑。应泰别号个园，园内又植竹万竿，所以题名"个园"，据刘凤诰所撰《个园记》："园系就寿芝园旧址重筑。"寿芝园原来叠石，相传为石涛所叠，但没有可靠的根据，或许因园中的黄石假山气势有似安徽的黄山，石涛善画黄山景，就附会是他的作品了。个园原来范围较现存要大些。现今住宅部分经维修后，仅存留中路与东路，大门及门屋已毁，照壁上的砖刻很精工。住宅各三进。正路大厅明间（当中的一间），减去两根"平柱"，这样它的开间就敞大了，应该说是当时为了兼作观戏之用才这样处理的。每进厅旁，都有套房小院，各院中置不同形式的花坛，竹影花香，十分幽静。园林在住宅的背面，从"火巷"（屋边小弄）中进入，有一株老干紫藤，浓荫深郁，人们到此便能得到一种清心悦目的感觉。往前左转达复道廊（两层的游廊），迎面左右有两个花坛，满植修竹，竹间放置了参差的石笋，用一真一假的处理手法，象征着春日山林。竹后花墙正中开一月洞门，上面题额是"个园"。门内为桂花厅，前面栽植丛桂，后面凿池，北面沿墙建楼七间，山连廊接，木映花承，登楼可鸟瞰全园。池的西面原有二舫，名"鸳鸯"。与此隔水相对耸立着六角亭。亭倒映池中，清澈如画。楼西叠湖石假山，名"秋云"（黄石秋山对景，故云），秀木繁荫，有松如盖。山下池水流入洞谷。渡过曲桥，有洞如屋，曲折幽邃，苍健夭矫，能发挥湖石形态多变的特征。因为洞屋较宽畅，洞口上部山石外挑，而水复流入洞中，兼以石色青灰，在夏日更觉凉爽。此处原有"十二洞"之称。假山正面向阳，湖石石面变化又多，尤其

an old wisteria tree casting shadows on the ground, refreshing visitors with its dark green color. Down the road on the left-hand side, there is a two-storied walkway, with two parterres on the left and the right sides, decorated with slender bamboos. Stones of various heights in the shape of bamboo shoots are planted in between the bamboos. The coupling of the real bamboos and the fake bamboo shoots represent the mountain forest in spring. The latticed wall behind the bamboos has a moon gate in the middle, with the name "Geyuan" inscribed above it. Behind the gate, there stands the Osmanthus Hall, decorated with sweet osmanthus bushes in the front and a pond in the back. Along the north wall there is a seven-bay storied building, which is next to the artificial mountain and connected with the walkway, surrounded by trees and flowers. Visitors get the aerial view of the garden at the top of the building. There used to be two painted land boats named "Yuanyang" (A Pair of Mandarin Ducks) at the west of the pond. They sat opposite a hexagonal pavilion across the pond, and the pavilion's reflection in clear water is as beautiful as a picture. To the west of the storied building is an artificial mountain made of Lake Tai stones and named "Qiuyun" (Autumn Cloud, named because it faces the Autumn Mountain of yellow stone). The mountain sits under the shade of flourishing trees, and a pine tree's crown form a canopy at the top. Under the mountain, a stream goes into a cave below. Passing through the zigzag bridge, there is a spacious cave shaped like a room, unexpectedly meandering and serenely deep, reflecting the diverse characteristics of Lake Tai stones. Stones project from the top of the cave, and the flowing water cools the gray-green cave in the summer. It is said there were twelve caves at this site. The front side of the artificial mountain faces the sun and its Lake Tai stones have various surfaces. Cast by sunshine, wind, and rain, the ever-changing shadows of the rockery mountain especially stun visitors in summer and is therefore aptly named Summer Mountain. Although the south of the mountain is empty and hollow today, it was planted with bamboos in the past. One can imagine its extraordinary scene with waving green bamboos, encircled by a whispering stream. The stairway in the Lake Tai mountain reaches top and then the seven-room storied building. Visitors reach the giant yellow mountain after passing through the seven-bay storied building, the corridor and the two-storied walkway. The mountain's front side faces the west. When the sun sets, a ray of red sunglow shines upon the yellow-stone mountain, highlighting its cliff and contrasting hues. The mountain rises up several dozen feet, high and steep into the clouds, looking like a painting of an autumn mountain and making it ideal for ascending a height in autumn. Just as what one does by designing the Spring Scenery and the Summer Mountain, craftsmen took advantage of different positions, orientations, materials and forms of the rocks to make the mountain stand out distinctively. Ancient cypresses grew out of stone chasms, whose rigid contours balance with the mountain's momentum, and green leaves and rough branches contrast with the ochre rocks. The method of planting cypresses to enhance the autumn scenery is in the same vein as planting bamboos for the Spring Scenery and pines for the Summer Mountain. All are deliberate design choices. The stairway sits

在夏日的阳光与风雨中，所起的阴影变化，更是好看，予人以夏山多态的感觉，因此称它为"夏山"。山南今很空旷，过去当为植竹的地方，想来万竿摇碧，流水湾环，又另生一番境界。从湖石山的磴道引登山巅，转至七间楼，经楼、廊与复道可到东首的黄石大假山。山的主面向西，每当夕阳西下，一抹红霞映照在黄石山上，不但山势显露，并且色彩倍觉醒目。而山的本身又拔地数丈，峻峭凌云，宛如一幅秋山图，是秋日登高的理想所在。它的设计手法与春景夏山同样，利用不同的地位、朝向、材料与山的形态达到各具特色的目的。山间有古柏出石隙中，使坚挺的形态与山势取得调和，苍绿的枝叶又与褐黄的山石造成对比。这与春景用竹、夏山用松一样，在植物的配置上，能从善于陪衬加深景色的角度出发，是经过一番选择与推敲的。磴道置于洞中，洞顶钟乳垂垂（以黄石倒悬代替钟乳石），天光隐隐从石窦中透入，人们在洞中上下盘旋，造奇致胜，构成了立体交通，发挥了黄石叠山的效果。山中还有小院、石桥、石室等与前者的综合运用，这又是别具一格的设计方法，在他处园林中尚是未见。山顶有亭，人在亭中见群峰皆置脚下。北眺绿杨城郭、瘦西湖、平山堂及观音山诸景，一一招入园内，是造园家极巧妙的手法，称为"借景"。山南有一楼，上下皆可通山。楼旁有一厅，厅的结构是用硬山式（建筑物只前后两坡用屋顶，两侧用山墙），迎面上悬姚正镛题"透风漏月"匾额。厅前堆白色雪石（宣石）假山，为冬日赏雪围炉的地方。因为要象征有雪意，将假山置于南面向北的墙下，看去有如积雪未消的样子。反之，如将雪石置于面阳的地方，则石中所含石英闪闪作光，就与雪意相违，这是叠雪石山时，不

inside the cave, in which stalactites hang from the roof (yellow stones take the place of stalactites) and skylight dimly penetrates through holes in the rocks. Visitors spiral around in the cave via a three-dimensional trail system, delighted by the sight of piling yellow stones to make a mountain. The comprehensive layout of small yards, stone bridges, stone chambers and the elements mentioned above is an unprecedented design methodology never seen before in other gardens. There is a pavilion on the top of the mountain, in which visitors see all the other mountains at their feet and the views of the city walls lined with green willows, Slender West Lake, Pingshan Hall, and Guanyin Mountain in the north. The method of incorporating views for spectators is a clever garden-making craft known as "view borrowing." A storied building to the south of the mountain is connected to the top and bottom of the mountain. A hall sits next to the storied building, whose structure features a traditional Chinese flush gable roof (the roof slopes down on the front and back sides, and gable walls are used on the right and left sides). A horizontal board hanging inside the hall is inscribed with its title "Toufeng-louyue" (Wind Filtering and Moonlight Permeable) written by Yao Zhengyong. There is a cluster of snow-white rocks (Xuan-stones) in front of the hall where residents used to gather around a fire to appreciate the winter snowfall. The rockery mountain is located at the foot of the north wall, facing the south because it is meant to resemble snow that has yet to thaw. If the mountain faces the sun, the quartz in it will glitter, which is against the winter atmosphere. Attention should be paid to these details while crafting white rockery mountains. Holes in the eastern wall let out the spring sceneries from the other side of the wall into the garden to suggest the "return of springtime to the world." The two-storied walkway to the garden atop the mountain no longer exists.

Geyuan Garden is famous for the intricacy of its rockery mountains. Early in the design stage, the garden's builder planned to exceed other gardens in Yangzhou by using all kinds of exceptional stones. His strategy of incorporating different stones for individual mountains was known as Four-Season Mountains, one of a kind among Chinese gardens. Though the Bayong (Eight Verses) Garden at Daliufang Xiang applied the same approach, the artificial mountains there did not have obvious peaks. Geyuan Garden stands out among Yangzhou's gardens. This particular kind of artificial mountain seems to summarize painters' concepts seen in Guo Xi's *Linquangaozhi* (*The Haughty and Uplifting Messages on Forests and Streams*), "The spring mountain should be subtly red like a smile; the summer mountain should be vigorously green as a drip of water; the autumn mountain should be bright and clear like a lady's make-up; the winter mountain should be so pale and bleak as if asleep." And from Dai Xi's *Xikuzhai Ti Hua* (*Colophons on Paintings of the Studio of Hard Working*), "The spring mountain is fit to be toured; the summer mountain is good for observation; the autumn mountain is great for ascending; the winter mountain is suitable as a dwelling."

能不注意的事。墙东列洞，引隔墙春景入院，借用"大地回春"的意思。上山可通入园的复道廊，但此复道廊已不存。

个园以假山堆叠的精巧而出名，在建造时就有超出扬州其他园林之上的意图，故以石斗奇，采取分峰用石的手法，号称"四季假山"，为国内唯一孤例。虽然大流芳巷八咏园也有同样的处理，不过没有起峰。这种假山似乎概括了画家所谓"春山淡冶而如笑，夏山苍翠而如滴，秋山明净而如妆，冬山惨淡而如睡"（见郭熙《林泉高致》）与"春山宜游，夏山宜看，秋山宜登，冬山宜居"（见戴熙《习苦斋题画》）的画埋，实为扬州园林中最具地方特色的一景。

## 寄啸山庄（116—135 页）

寄啸山庄在花园巷，今名"何园"，清光绪间官僚做道台的何芷舠所筑，为清代扬州大型园林的最后作品。由住宅可达园内，园后刁家巷另设一门，当时是为招待外客的出入口。住宅建筑除楠木厅外，都是洋房，楼横堂列，廊庑回缭，在平面布局上，尚具中国传统。从宅中最后一进墙上的什锦空窗（砖框）中隐约地能见到园的一角。园中为大池。池北楼宽七楹，因主楼三间稍突，两侧楼平舒展伸，屋角又都起翘，有些像蝴蝶的形式，当地人叫做"蝴蝶厅"。楼旁连复道廊可绕全园，高低曲折，人行其间有随势凌空的感觉，而中部与东部又用此复道廊作为分隔，人们的视线通过上下壁间的漏窗，可互见两面景色，显得空灵深远。这是中国园林利用分隔扩大空间面积的手法之一。此园运用这一

**Jixiao Shanzhuang** (Page 116-135)

Jixiao Shanzhuang at Huayuan Xiang is known as the Ho Family Garden or He Garden today. He Zhidao, a circuit intendant under the Guangxu reign, built the garden, which is the last large-scale garden dating back to the Qing Dynasty. The garden is accessible from the residence, and there is another door for visitors in the back of the garden at Diaojia Xiang. The residential buildings adopt a western style, except for a hall built of *Phoebe nanmu*. However, the layout of the residence is still traditionally Chinese as the halls and storied buildings are laid out in rows and columns, surrounded by roofed walkways. From the brick-framed latticed windows in the wall of the last row of the houses, one can see a corner of the garden. There is a big pond in the garden. A seven-bay storied building sits at the north of the pond whose three central bays slightly extrude out. It streches on both sides and the eaves on the ends lift up. Since the building looks like a butterfly, local residents call it "Butterfly Hall." The two-storied walkway surrounding the building leads to the whole garden at different levels, making those walking in it feel as though they are ascending and descending in the sky. The same walkway is also used to separate the central and eastern sections of the garden. The garden thus looks spacious and deep, and visitors get to see the scenery of both sides through the latticed windows. Here, the garden naturally and effectively uses the Chinese garden's strategy of spatial separation to extend visitors' views. To the east of the pond, a square pavilion surrounded by water allows visitors to cool themselves and enjoy Kunqu Opera. This pavilion takes advantage of echoes of the water to enhance acoustic effects and also uses the encircling walkway as the seats for the audience. In feudal society, female audience members could only sit in the two-storied walkway closer to the garden and watch through translucent curtains from window opening of different shapes in the wall. Today, the strategy of constructing the pavilion by the water to enhance acoustic effects is still viable, though the audience area in the walkway and behind the windows and curtain are eliminated. Latticed windows enhance the viewer's perception of the garden's layers and variation. This is an effective technique, as a common Chinese saying states that "sceneries and views can hardly be locked up by a small open window." An artificial mountain sits at the southwestern corner of the pond, and the West Veranda is hidden behind the mountain, with a raised flowerbed of arboreous peony to the south. Together, they undulate with the mountain terrain and appear quite natural. This technique is simple, unpretentious, and easy to integrate into newly constructed gardens. The moutain can be climbed through a stone stairway, which then leads to a cave. The cave appears mysterious deep and the moutain dangerous tall. The yellow-stone mountain and the Lake Tai stone stairway are built of different kinds of material but can still be appreciated as a whole. Together, they twist and turn in an elegant style. There is a cave with water at the eastern foot of the mountain. The cave seems interesting except that it could be improved as it has one end connected with a column. To the south of the mountain is a three-bay storied building, whose front sits a rugged peak. Visitors can reach the top of the building through a stairway and to the two-storied walkway in the east to reach the residential part of the estate. The

手法，较为自如而特出。池东筑水亭，四角卧波，为纳凉拍曲的地方。此戏亭利用水面的回音，增加音响效果，又利用回廊作为观剧的看台。在封建社会，女宾只能坐在宅内贴园的复道廊中，通过疏帘，从墙上的什锦空窗中观看。这种临水筑台，增强音响效果的手法今天还可以酌予采取，而复道廊隔帘观剧的看台是要扬弃的。如用空窗引景、泄景，以加深园林层次与变化，当然还是一种有效的手法，所谓"景物锁难小牖通"便是形容这种境界。池西南角为假山，山后隐西轩，轩南的牡丹台，随着山势层叠起伏，看去十分自然，这种做法并不费事，而又平易近人，无矫揉做作之态，新建园林中似可推广。越山穿洞，洞幽山危，黄石山壁与湖石磴道尚宛转多姿，虽用不同的石类，却能浑然一体。山东麓有一水洞，略具深意，唯一头与柱相交接，稍嫌考虑不周。山南崇楼三间，楼前峰峦嶙峋，经山道可以登楼，向东则转入住宅复道廊。复道廊为叠落形（屋顶顺次作阶段高低），有游廊与复廊（一条廊中用墙分隔为二）两种形式，墙上开漏窗，巧妙地分隔成中东两部。漏窗以水磨砖对缝构成，面积很大，图案简洁，手法挺秀工整。廊东有四面厅，与三间轩相对设置。院中碧梧倚峰，荫翳蔽日。阶下花街铺地（用鹅石子与碎砖瓦等拼花铺成的地面）与厅前砖砌栏凳，极为相称，它和漏窗一样，亦为别处所不及，是具有地方风格的一种艺术品。厅后的假山贴墙而筑，壁岩与磴道无率直之弊，假山体形不大，尚能含蓄寻味，尤其是小亭踞峰，旁倚粉墙之下，加之古木掩映，每当夕阳晚照，碎影满阶，成就了中国园林以白粉墙为底产生虚实的景色。虽然面积不大，但景物的变化万千，在小

walkway is stacking and stepping (its roof goes up and down in coherence with the height of the buildings) with two forms: single lane or double lane (a single lane separated into two lanes with a wall in the middle). The estate is skillfully divided into central and eastern sections by walls with latticed windows. The windows are constructed of finely-ground bricks, which are quite large and fit together to form simple and succinct patterns. A hall with windows on four sides sits at the east of the walkway, facing the three-bay storied building. Inside the court, a green Chinese parasol tree leans against the mountain and blocks the sunshine with its lush leaves. The ground at the foot of the stairway has a flowery pattern pavement (a mixture of cobbles, broken bricks, and tiles), which are harmonious with the brick railings and benches in front of the hall. Surpassing the handicrafts in other places, the pavement is a successful art style with vernacular characteristics, such as the latticed windows. A rockery mountain leans upon the back wall of the hall, and the mountain surface merges well with the stone stairway. The rockery mountain is not overly large, but offers interesting scenary. The scene includes the mountain standing beside the white-washed wall, and a tiny pavilion sitting at its top. The garden nests under ancient trees' green branches. When the sun sets, broken shadows cover the entire stone stairway, producing an image of the real and surreal, against a white-washed wall as the background in a traditional Chinese garden. Though the setting is not grand, the scenery within is ever-changing. This is an effective strategy for tight spaces. The stone stairway northwest of the mountain leads to a terrace on the two-storied walkway. With the old terrace at the west end of the walkway, these two places were ideal for moon-gazing, particularly at moonrise and moonset. Regarding plants, sweet osmanthus trees were planted in the mountain in front of the hall. Arboreous and herbaceous peonies were planted in parterres. There are lacebark pines at the mountain's foot, Chinese parasol trees in front of the stairway, and plantains added at the corners. All the plants are planted in batches so they are verdant and pleasant. In spring, they flourish with colors. In summer, they form large, cooling shadows. In autumn, they diffuse heavy fragrance. In winter, the plants remain dark green. The seasonal scenes were thoughtfully arranged, based on each plants' character and local conditions. This garden is known for its spaciousness and robust character. Water and rocks are arranged to complement the buildings, making the mountain's color and water's light stay in contrasts with the storied buildings and corridors. In all, they form an interesting image of emptiness and solidity. The main halls are linked and segmented by two-storied walkway and artificial mountains, and the arteries and veins of the garden exist by themselves up and down. Therefore, the garden is a three-dimensional communication network that can be enjoyed at multiple levels. The scenery surface spreads out around the water. Walls with latticed windows construct infinite views of lofts, terraces, flowers and trees shimmering between the partitions. The garden was constructed rather late, so new materials and patterns were utilized during construction. In addition, there was also an additional gate to greet guests. Compared to older gardens, its layout is more spacious and smooth; visitors can transition from static appreciation to dynamic sightseeing. The garden's paths are sometimes circuitous and other times

空间的院落中，还是一种可取的手法。山西北有磴道，拾级可达楼层复道廊中的半月台，它与西部复道廊尽端楼层的旧有半月台分别是用来观看月升与月落的。在植物配置方面，厅前山间栽桂，花坛种牡丹、芍药，山麓植白皮松，阶前植梧桐，转角补芭蕉，均以群植为主，因此葱翠宜人。春时绚烂，夏日浓荫，秋季馥郁，冬令苍青，都有规律可循，就不同植物特性因地制宜而安排。此园以开畅雄健见长，水石用来衬托建筑物，使山色水光与崇楼杰阁、复道修廊相映成趣，虚实互见。又以厅堂为主，以复道廊与假山贯串分隔，上下脉络自存，形成立体交通的多层欣赏的园林。它的风景面环水展开，而花墙分隔构成了深深不尽的景色，楼台花木，隐现其间。此园建造时期较晚，装修已多新材料与新纹样，又另辟园门可招待外客等，其格局更是较之过去的为宏畅，使游

者由静观的欣赏渐趋动观的游览。透
迤衡直，闿爽深密，都深具中国园林
的特征，造园手法亦有一定程度的推
陈出新。

## 小盘谷（136—143 页）

　　小盘谷在大树巷，清光绪二十年
（1894）后，由官僚两江、两广总督
周馥购自徐姓重修而成，至民国初年
复经修整。园在宅的东部，自大厅旁
入月门，额名"小盘谷"，从笔意看来，
似出陈鸿寿[6]之手。花厅三间，面山
作曲尺形，游者绕到厅后，忽见一池
汪洋，豁然开朗。厅侧有水阁枕流，
以游廊相接，它与隔岸山石，隐约花
墙，形成一种中国园林中惯用的以建
筑物与自然景物对比的手法。廊前有
曲桥达对岸，桥尽入幽洞，洞很广，
内置棋桌，利用穴窦采光。复临水辟
门，人自此可循阶至池。洞左通步石
（用石块置水中代桥）、崖道，导至

straightforward. Its sceneries are sometimes wide open, and other times mysterious and profound. These inventive and innovative strategies are all representative of Chinese gardens.

### Xiaopangu (Page 136-143)

Xiaopangu at Dashu Xiang was originally owned by someone surnamed Xu, and later acquired and renovated by Zhou Fu, viceroy of present-day Jiangsu, Anhui, Jiangxi, Guangdong and Guangxi provinces after 1894, the 20th year of the Guangxu reign of the Qing Dynasty. It was renovated again in the early Republican years. The garden is located in the eastern part of the estate, entering from the moon gate by the side of its main hall. The name "Xiaopangu" engraved in the board seems to be the handwriting of Chen Hongshou[6] . The three-bay parlor facing the mountain is in the shape of a carpenter's ruler. When visitors move to the back of the parlor, a pond of clear water emerges in sight. Beside the parlor, a belvedere sitting above the water is connected to a meandering walkway. It contrasts with the mountains and rockeries across the water, and the latticed wall that can be seen indistinctly. The strategy of contrasting buildings and scenery is common to Chinese gardens. In front of the walkway, a zigzag bridge leads to a cave on the other side of the water. Light penetrates the cave through apertures in the ceiling to illuminate a chess table inside it. From the cave, one can again reach the pond through a door and stone steps by the water. To the left of the cave, stepping stones (planted in the water instead of a bridge) and a trail lead to the parlor in the back. A stone stairway in front of the parlor provides access to the top of the mountain. These elements compose the entrance to the valley, which is named "Shuiliu-yunzai" (Water

Flows Where Clouds Are). The design of the cave is a very good example of constructing mountain caves—spacious, but also zigzagging with plenty of variation. Turning right to exit the cave, visitors enter the small courtyard. Then, turning upward, they enter a meandering corridor, which eventually leads to the peak of the mountain. A pavilion named Wind Pavilion sits at the top of the mountain, where visitors get the view of both the eastern and western parts of the estate. Nowadays, the eastern part's layout, previously destroyed, is under renovation. The pavilion's entrance is a peach-shaped door, whose lintel is inscribed with "Congcui" (Clustered Greenary). The hall in the shape of a carpenter's square at the north of the pond has been rebuilt. The nine-meter-tall mountain is lofty and rugged in shape, titled as "Jiushitushan" (Mountain of Nine-Lion Picture). Unfortunately, the original shape of the mountain was disrupted during early Republican repairments. Still, this rockery mountain is one of the best examples of its kind among all gardens in Yangzhou. Rockeries, mountains, water ponds, and buildings are all laid out together with clear contrast on a rather cramped piece of land. The whole garden evokes a sense of mysterious fantasy with striking contrasts between buildings and rockeries, rockeries and white-washed walls, rockeries and pond, front yard and back garden, depth and openness, height and flatness, and so on. The latticed walls are segmented in a random manner. The location of the mountain, the stone walls, stepping stones, and the entrance of the valley are carefully chosen so that the stiff mountain shoulders the verdant branches, the gray rocks face the clear stream, the stones accompany the water, and everything is in harmony within the

后部花厅，厅前山尽头有磴道可上山，这里是一个很好的谷口，题为"水流云在"。山洞的处理既开敞又曲折多变化，应该说是构筑山洞的好实例。右出洞转入小院，向上折入游廊，可登山巅。山上有亭名"风亭"，坐亭中可以顾盼东西两部的景色，今东部布置已毁，正在修复中。其入口门作桃形，额为"丛翠"。池北曲尺形厅，今改建。山拔地峥嵘，名"九狮图山"，峰高约9米，惜民国初年修缮时，略损原状。此园假山为扬州诸园中的上选作品。山石水池与建筑物皆集中处理，对比明显，用地紧凑，以建筑物与山石、山石与粉墙、山石与水池、前院与后园、幽深与开朗、高峻与低平等对比手法，形成一时难分的幻景。花墙间隔得非常灵活，山峦、石壁、步石、谷口等相叠置，正是危峰耸翠，苍岩临流，水石交融，浑然一片，其妙处在于运用"以少胜多"的艺术手法。虽然园内没有崇楼与复道廊，但是幽曲多姿，浅画成图。廊屋皆不髹饰，以木材的本色出之。叠山的技术尤佳，足与苏州环秀山庄抗衡，显然出于名匠师之手，按清光绪《江都县续志》卷十二记片石山房云："园以湖石胜，石为狮九，有玲珑天骄之概。"[7]今从小盘谷假山章法分析，似以片石山房为蓝本，并参考其他佳作综合提高而成。又据《扬州画舫录》卷二云："淮安董道士叠九狮山，亦藉藉人口。"卷六又云："卷石洞天在城闉清梵之后……以旧制临水太湖石山，搜岩剔穴为九狮形，置之水中，上点桥亭，题之曰'卷石洞天'。"扬州博物馆藏李斗书九狮山条幅，盛谷跋语指为卷石洞天九狮山，但未言系董道士所叠。据旧园主周叔弢丈及其侄煦良先生说，小盘谷的假山一向以"九狮图山"相沿称，由来已久，想系定有所据。因此，我认为当时九狮山在扬州必不

scene. All the elements are integrated as a whole and emphasize the artistic approach of "less is more." The garden is serene and meandering, with many beautiful characteristics, although there are no lofty buildings or storied walkways. The rooms are not painted or decorated elaborately, but instead feature the original surface of the timber. The technique of artificial mountain construction is comparable to Huanxiu Shanzhuang in Suzhou. It is no doubt that the rockeries are piled up by a master craftsman. According to vol.12 of *Jiangdu Xian Xu Zhi* (*The Sequel to the Gazetteer of Jiangdu County*), compiled under the Guangxu reign of the Qing Dynasty, Pianshi Shanfang "is famous for its Lake Tai rocks in the shape of nine lions, which is so exquisite that looks like the mountain came from heaven."[7] Judging from the compositional techniques applied at the artificial mountain in Xiaopangu, Pianshi Shanfang is the chief inspiration, and also learnt from other gardens. According to vol.2 of *Yangzhou Huafang Lu*, "Everyone in town is talking about the Jiushishan (Nine-Lion Mountain) crafted by Taoist Dong from Huai'an." And from vol.6, "Juanshi Dongtian (Rolling Stone Cave) sits behind the Chengyin Qingfan (Huiyin Temple by the Northern City Wall)...From an old style rockery of Lake Tai stones that sits by the water, the master added new holes to the original ones to make the rocks into the shape of nine lions, which he then placed in the pond, added a bridge with a pavilion on the top, and named it 'Juanshi Dongtian.'" The calligraphy scroll *Jiushishan* written by Li Dou and collected in the Yangzhou Museum was once commented by Sheng Gu, who indicate that Jiushishan is located at Juanshi Dongtian but does not claim that Taoist Dong is the mind behind the rockeries. According to the garden's former owners Zhou Shutao and his nephew Zhou Xuliang, the artificial mountain of Xiaopangu has always been called "Jiushitushan" (Mountain of Nine-Lion Picture) from long time ago. They think there must be reasons behind. Therefore, I believe there must have been more than one Jiushishan in Yangzhou at that time, and the one at Juanshi Dongtian was the most famous one. Taoist Dong was famous for piling up similar mountains of this kind, which became a trend by itself. Taoist Dong lived in the Qianlong reign. Nowadays, it is accepted that the peak, the cave, the trail, the mountain against wall, the stepping stones, the valley entrance, and other techniques of this moutain all came from the same time period. In addition, the horizontal board inscribed by Chen Hongshou was dated near this time period as well. For now, I propose that even if the mountain was not constructed by Taoist Dong himself, it must have been done by imitating his technique. Another Xiaopangu in Qin's Yiyuan Garden, located at Tangzi Xiang near the Old City's South Gate, was a miniature yellow-stone mountain built after the Qianlong reign by the master gardener Ge Yuliang from Changzhou. Now, it no longer exists. Vol.12 of *Lüyuan Conghua* describes the master gardener, "Lately, a Changzhou native named Ge Yuliang excels in artificial mountain construction than all others." So, Ge's time period is later than Taoist Dong. Judging from the ruins of the Qin's Xiaopangu, the mountain seems plain and implicit with a "female" style; whereas this Xiaopangu represents masculine features with its lofty peak and magnificent appearence. These two master craftsmen for rockeries were both visitors to Yangzhou. Their two representative works brought them equal shares of honor.

止一处，而以卷石洞天为最出名。董道士以叠此类假山而著名，其后渐渐形成了一种风气。董道士是乾隆间人。今证以峰峦、洞曲、崖道、壁岩、步石、谷口等，皆这一时期的手法，而陈鸿寿所书一额，时间又距离不太远，姑且提出这个假设：即使不是董道士的原作，亦必模拟其手法而成。旧城南门堂子巷的秦氏意园小盘谷系黄石堆叠的假山小品，乾隆以后所筑，出名匠师常州戈裕良之手，今不存。《履园丛话》卷十二载："近时有戈裕良者，常州人，其堆法尤胜于诸家。"据此，则戈氏时期略迟于董道士。从秦氏小盘谷遗迹来看，山石平淡蕴藉，以"阴柔"出之，而此小盘谷则高险磅礴，似以"阳刚"制胜。这两位叠山名手同时作客扬州，那么，这两件艺术作品正是他们的颉颃之作，用以平分秋色了。

## 逸圃（144—147页）

　　东关街个园的西首，有园名"逸圃"，为李姓的宅园。从大门入，迎面有洞门，额书"逸圃"二字。左转为住宅。月门内有廊修直，在东墙叠山，委婉屈曲，壁岩森严，与墙顶之瓦花墙形成虚实对比。山旁筑牡丹台，花时若锦。山间北头的尽端，倚墙筑五边形半亭，亭下有碧潭，清澈可以照人。花厅三间南向，装修极精，外廊天花，皆施浅雕。厅后小轩三间，带东厢配以西廊，前置花木山石。轩背置小院，设门而常关，初看去与木壁无异。沿磴道可达复廊，即由楼后转入隔园，园在住宅之后，以复道与山石相连，折向西北，有东向楼三间，面峰而筑。楼有盘楼可下，旁有紫藤一架，老干若虬，满阶散绿，增色不少。此园与苏州曲园相仿佛，都是利用曲尺形隙地加以布置，但比曲园巧妙，形成上下错综，境界多变。匠师们在

## Yipu (Page 144-147)

　　To the west of Geyuan Garden on Dongguan Street, there is Yipu, the residence and garden of the Li Family. Entering the front entrance, there is a door opening, with the name "Yipu" inscribed on the top. Turning left, there is the residence. Inside the gate, there is a narrow and straight corridor. Against the east wall, artificial mountains twist and turn, which look solid and forbidding, in contrast with the latticed windows near the top of the wall. Beside the mountain, there is a raised flowerbed of arboreous peony. In full bloom, they are as gorgeous as brocade. At the northern end of the mountain, a half pentagonal pavilion leans against the wall. A mirror-like pond sits under the pavilion. Facing south, a three-bay parlor is exquisitely decorated and the ceiling of its exterior corridor is fully carved in relief. Behind the parlor, there is a three-bay veranda with an eastern wing and western corridor, and in the front, there are flowers, trees and rockeries. A small courtyard sits at the back of the veranda, which has a locked door, and it looks like a wooden wall at first sight. A stone stairway is connected to a two-storied walkway that runs along the back of a storied building, turning into the garden that is located behind the residential area. The rockery mountain in the garden is connected with two-storied walkways. When it turns into the northwestern corner, a three-bay storied building facing east is constructed against a rockery mountain. Visitors can exit the building from the top down through a spiral staircase. Beside the staircase, a pergola of wisteria add sophistication to the garden with its entangled branches and green leaves fallen on the steps. This garden is similar to the Quyuan Garden in Suzhou;

both have small sites in the shape of a carpenter's square. However, this garden's layout is even more ingenious. The sceneries are ever-changing, with intricate touring route. While gardeners laid out this garden, they used the strategy called "rescued from desperation": the tiny courtyard is connected to the neighboring garden, which makes the courtyard seems infinite. This typology is common among other gardens in the history, thereby making it a feature of Yangzhou landscape architecture.

**Yilu (Page 148-149)**

Yilu is the parlor area of Huang's residence (the residence of a banker named Huang Yizhi) at Jijiawan, and the work of Yu Jizhi. Master Yu's strength lies in both rockery mountain construction and floral art. He is especially good at piling up rockeries for small gardens. The parlor area is comprised of two rows of buildings. In front of and behind the first row, there are both small yards. The eastern and southern sides of the front yard are lined with corridors, and a snow-white stone sits at the western side, shadowed by a sweet osmanthus tree. At the back of the first row, there are two wings, and the parterres in the back yard are planted with bamboos and stone-made bamboo shoots. When the leaves sway, visitors feel engulfed by greenery. The west part of the parlor area is partitioned by a latticed wall, in which a moon gate leads to an inner yard with a suite of chambers. The latticed wall creates an illusion of depth of the courtyards. Because of the view-browing from the outside yard, the inner yard appears larger than it is. Using separation to increase the space is a common strategy in Chinese architecture, and here is a good example of gardens inside residences. The back row has

设计此园时，利用"绝处逢生"的手法，凭借由小院转入隔园的办法，营造一个似尽而未尽的布局。这种情况在过去扬州园中并不少见，亦为扬州园特色之一。

## 怡庐（148—149 页）

怡庐是稽家湾黄宅（银钱商黄益之宅）花厅的一部分，系余继之的作品。余工叠山，善艺花卉，小园点石尤为能手。怡庐花厅计二进。前进的前后皆列小院，院中东南两面筑廊，西面则点雪石一丘，荫以丛桂。厅后翼两厢，小院的花坛上配石笋修竹，枝叶纷披，人临其间有滴翠分绿的感觉。厅西隔花墙，自月门中入，有套房内院，它给外院造成了"庭院深深深几许"的景色，又因外院的借景，而内院中便显得小中见大了。这是中国建筑中用分隔增大空间的手法，是现有居住的院落中较好的例子。后厅三间，面对山石，其西亦置套房小院。从平面论，此小园无甚出人意料处，但建筑物与院落比例匀当，装修亦以横线条出之，使空间宽绰有余，而点石栽花，亦能恰到好处。至于大小院落的处理，又能发挥其密处见疏，静中生趣的优点，从这里可见绿化及空间组合对小型建筑的重要性。

## 余园（150—152页）

余园在广陵路，初名"陇西后圃"，清光绪年间归刘姓盐商后，就旧园修筑而成，又名"刘庄"，因曾设怡大钱庄于此，一般称"怡大花园"。园位住宅之后，以院落分隔，前院南向为厅，其西缀以廊屋，墙下筑湖石花坛，有白皮松二株。厅后一院，西端多修竹，墙下叠黄石山，由磴道可登楼。东院有楼，北向筑，其下凿池叠山，而湖石壁岩，尤为这园精华之所在。

three bays facing the rockeries, and on the west side, there is also suite of chambers and inner yard. Judging from the site plan, there is nothing particularly unique regarding this small garden; however, the buildings and the gardens are laid out in proportion, and the interior decoration is governed by a horizontal grid that enhances the spaciousness. In addition, the rockeries and flowers are in just the right place and amount. And regarding the treatment of the large and small yards, they are well-spaced even in crowded areas, presenting vivacious atmosphere in a quiet place. This small garden is a clear demonstration of the importance of greenery and spatial composition.

### Yuyuan Garden (Page 150-152)

Yuyuan Garden is located on Guangling Road and was originally named as "Longxi Houpu" (Back Garden of Longxi). During the Guangxu reign of the Qing Dynasty, a merchant surnamed Liu acquired the land and built on top of the old architecture, so it is also called "Liuzhuang" (Liu's Manor). Moreover, since the Yida Money Shop was located here, the garden is commonly known as Yida Garden. The garden sits behind the residence and is divided into several yards. The front yard has a hall facing south, whose west side is linked to corridors and buildings. A parterre built of Lake Tai stones are situated at the foot of the wall, with two lacebark pine trees planted alongside it. The back yard sits behind the hall, with plenty of slender bamboos on the western end. A yellow-stone rockery mountain is piled up at the bottom of the wall, and a stone stairway provides access to the top of the building. There is a north-facing storied building in the east yard, overlooking artificial mountains and a pond, and there's Lake Tai stone mountain built against the wall, which is the essence of the garden.

### Weipu (Page 153-155)

Weipu owned by the Chen Family is at Fengxiang Xiang. Entering by the southeastern corner, there are artificial mountains in the yard, which is full of greenery with aged wisteria vines and an old cypress. Though there are only a few rocks against the wall, they are in various forms of caves and peaks. The view of the garden from the north hall is rather impressive. Walkways are along the east and the west sides. A waterside pavilion is constructed at the southwestern corner, with a refreshing fish pond at its foot. The garden's layout is simple, but harmonious.

### Yangshi Xiaozhu

Beside Weipu is Yangshi Xiaozhu (Yang's Small Alcove). As its name implies, it is a small corner garden originally belonging to the parlor's studio. The garden sits in front of the two-bay parlor, decorated with a few rocks and bamboos, and separated by a latticed wall. At the side of the garden, a diagonal corridor provides access to a small belvedere. In front of the belvedere, there is a small pond of water among the rocks. The garden owner is keen on orchids, so potted orchids are the focus of the garden; no other plants and flowers were allowed to overcome the orchids' fragrance. Though this place can hardly be considered as a garden, it has a complete layout and the appropriate segmentation of the front and back. Visitors do not feel cramped at all in this tiny garden; instead, they enjoy gazing at the surrounding sceneries.

## 蔚圃（153—155 页）

陈氏蔚圃在风箱巷。东南角入门，院中置假山，配以古藤老柏，很觉苍翠葱郁，假山仅墙下少许，然有洞可寻，有峰可赏，自北部厅中望去，景物森然。东西两面配游廊，西南角则建水榭，下映鱼池，多清新之感。这小院布置虽寥寥数事，却甚得体。

## 杨氏小筑

蔚圃旁有杨氏小筑，真可谓"一角的小园"，原属花厅书斋部分。入门为花厅两间，前列小院，点缀少量山石竹木，以花墙分隔，旁有斜廊，上达小阁，阁前山石间有水一泓，因地位过小，以鱼缸聚水，配合很觉相称。园主善艺兰，此小园平时以盆兰为主花，故不以绚丽花木而夺其芬芳。此处虽不足以园称，然园的格局具备，前后分隔得宜，咫尺的面积，能无局促之感，反觉多左右顾盼生景的妙处。

扬州园林的主人，以富商为多，他们除拥有盘剥得来的物质财富外，还捐得一个空头的官衔，以显耀其身份；因此，这些园林在设计的主导思想上与官僚地主的园林有了些不同。最特出的地方便是一味追求豪华，借以炫富有，榜风雅。在清康熙、乾隆年间，正如上述所说的还期望能得到皇帝的"御赏"，以达到升官发财的目的，若干处还模拟一些皇家园林的手法；因此，在园林的总面貌上，建筑物的尺度、材料的品类都向高敞华丽方面追求，即以楼厅面阔而论，有多至七间的。其他楼层复道，巨峰名石，以及分峰用石的四季假山（个园、八咏园）和积土累石的"斗鸡台"（壶园有此），更因多数富商为安徽徽州府属人，间有模拟皖南山水者。建筑用的木材，佳者选用楠木。楼层铺方砖。地面除鹅石的"花街"外，院中有用大理石的。至于装修陈设的华丽

Owners of Yangzhou gardens are mostly rich merchants. In addition to acquiring material wealth from business, they also bought nominal official titles to display their status. Therefore, these gardens' leading design concepts are different from gardens owned by bureaucratic landlords. The most significant difference lies in their excessive pursuit of extravagance and luxury to display their wealth. During the Kangxi and Qianlong reigns of the Qing Dynasty, as mentioned earlier, some merchants created gardens, in expectation of the emperor's inspection bringing them wealth and official titles. They even imitate techniques of royal gardens in some places. As a result, the gardens' configuration, size, and building materials were lavish and striking. Regarding spaciousness, some storied halls have up to seven bays; buildings and walkways have multiple floors; large rockery mountains are built of famous stones; and artificial mountains at Geyuan Garden and Bayong Garden have different rocks for peaks to represent the four seasons; there are even a gamecock arena built by piling up soils and stones in Huyuan Garden. Moreover, since most Yangzhou merchants were Anhui natives, some gardens evoked the landscape of south Anhui. In terms of material, the preferable choice was *Phoebe nanmu*. Floors were paved with square bricks. The paths are paved with pebbles to from various patterns and courtyards are sometimes paved with marble. The lavish interior decoration represented the garden owners' desire to enjoy "poetic" and "picturesque" landscapes, to display their decadent lifestyle, and also to transform the gardens into social places for large gatherings. Therefore, though they share the same design concept as Suzhou gardens, Yangzhou gardens are also designed for a social purpose. This kind of design intent is easily seen in large gardens such as Geyuan Garden, Jixiao Shanzhuang and so on. The Yangzhou school of verse and prose and the Eight Eccentrics' styles of painting are more bold and unconstrained than those of Suzhou. This freer style influenced and enhanced Yangzhou's gardens to some extent. In order to understand Yangzhou's gardens, the garden owners' resources and demands must be examined. The above mentioned objective and subjective conditions determined design prerequisites and design concepts, influencing conception and style of the gardens.

Different natural environment and material choices influenced gardens' style to a certain extent. With a flat terrain, moderate soil humidity, mild climate and modest rainfall, Yangzhou has the strengths of both south and north China. The environment is fertile for flowers and trees, especially arboreous and herbaceous peonies, which is advantageous for luxurious gardens. The rocks used to pile up artificial mountains were mostly shipped by salt-shipping boats from sites near, such as Zhenjiang, Gaozi, Jurong, Suzhou, Yixing,

等都反映了园主除享受所谓"诗情画意"的山水景色与炫富斗财的意图外，还有为招待较多的宾客作为交际场所之意，因此它与苏州园林在同一设计主导思想下还多了这一层用意。这种设计思想在大型的园林如个园、寄啸山庄等最容易见到。扬州的诗文与"扬州八怪"的画风在风格上亦比吴门派来得豪放深厚，这些多少给造园带来了一定影响。要研究扬州园林，无疑必须先弄清这些园主当时的物质力量与精神需要。这些主、客观因素决定了园林设计的要求与主导思想，因而影响了园林的意境与风格。

自然环境与材料的不同对园林的风格是有一定影响的。扬州地势平坦，土壤干湿得宜，气候及雨量亦适中，兼有南北两地的长处；所以，花木易于滋长，而芍药、牡丹尤为茂盛。这对豪华的园林来说，是最有利的条件。叠山所用的石材多利用盐船回载，近则取自江浙的镇江、高资、句容、苏州、宜兴、吴兴、武康等地，远则运自皖赣的徽州府属：宣城、灵璧、湖口等处，更有少量奇峰异石是罗致西南诸省的，因此，石材的品种要比苏州所用为多。

中国园林的建造总是利用"因地制宜"的原则，尤其在水网与山陵地带。可是，扬州属江淮平原，水位不太高，土地亦坦旷，因此在规划园林时，与苏杭一带利用天然地形与景色就有所不同了。多数大型园林中部为池，厅堂又为一园的主体，两者必相配合；池旁筑山，点缀亭阁，周联复道，以花墙、山石、树木为园林的间隔，造成有层次富变化的景色。这可以个园、寄啸山庄为代表。中小型园林则倚墙叠山石，下辟水池，适当地辅以游廊水榭，结构比较紧凑。片石山房、小盘谷都按这个原则配置而成。

Wuxing, and Wukang in Jiangsu and Zhejiang, and far, such as Xuancheng, Lingbi, and Hukou in Anhui and Jiangxi. Some exotic rocks came as far as southwestern China, resulting in more varieties of rocks in Yangzhou gardens than Suzhou.

Chinese garden construction follows the principle of "building to local standards," especially in areas crisscrossed with rivers or in hilly land. Being part of Yangtze-Huai basin, Yangzhou's water level is low and the land is open. When planning gardens, garden designers are not able to take advantage of natural topography and sceneries as in Suzhou. Oftentimes, there is a pond at the center of large gardens, and a hall is the main feature of the garden. The pond and the hall must coordinate with each other. Rockery mountains sit beside the pond and pavilions and belvederes are scattered but connected by walkways. Latticed walls, mountains, and trees separate the gardens to create multi-layered and varied views. Geyuan Garden and Jixiao Shanzhuang are good examples. Medium and small-sized gardens are in general more compact. Rockery mountains with ponds at the foot are piled up by the walls, and corridors and waterside pavilions are properly located. Pianshi Shanfang and Xiaopangu are laid out following such principle. According to the remaining area of the residence or the size of the courtyard, a few rockeries, a small fish pond, a waterside pavilion, a raised flowerbed of arboreous peony or a nursery of herbaceous peony are laid out nicely, without being overcrowded, resulting in a bright and pleasant feeling. Weipu and the Yangshi Xiaozhu are great examples. Yipu is another example of a garden planned in a narrow space in the shape of a carpenter's square, demonstrating the many variations within this layout. In summary, Yangzhou gardens are relatively flat in plan, with a combination of static appreciation and dynamic sightseeing for the visitors. The success lies in the three-dimensional traffic and multi-layered viewing routes such as two-storied walkways, storied buildings, belvederes, and caves in artificial mountains. Caves, stone houses, and stone chambers are all interconnected and offer various views. However, certain features are not perfect. Water, rocks and buildings are not thoroughly blended. Most shorelines are too straight, lacking bends and turns. Flat stones projecting over the water or water flow over stones are hardly seen anywhere. Gardens such as Pianshi Shanfang, Xiaopangu, and the foothills of Yipu and the Qiuyun Mountain in Geyuan Garden are cases overcame imperfections. There is also a technique to make "dry garden with water." An example would be Erfenmingyue (Two-Thirds Bright Moonlight) Tower builted by an officer surnamed Yuan in the Daoguang reign of the Qing Dynasty (the name of the building was written by Qian Yongshu). The ground is lowered so that the hall

庭院根据住宅余地面积的多寡或院落的大小安排少许假山立峰，旁凿小鱼池，筑水榭，或布置牡丹台、芍药圃，内容并不求多，便能给人以一种明净宜人的感觉。蔚圃与杨氏小筑即为其例，而逸圃又是利用狭长曲尺形隙地构成平面布局较多变化的一个突出的例子。总的说来，扬州园林在平面布局上较为平整，动观与静观相结合，然其妙处在于立体交通与多层观赏线，如复道廊、楼、阁以及假山的窦穴。洞曲、山房、石室，皆能上下沟通，自然变化多端了，但就水面与山石、建筑相互发挥作用来说，未能做到十分交融——驳岸多数似较平直，少曲折湾环，而石矶、石濑等几乎不见亦是美中不足的地方。但从片石山房、小盘谷及逸圃、个园"秋云"山麓来看，则尚多佳处。又有"旱园水做"的办法，如广陵路清道光年间建的员姓"二分明月楼"（钱泳书额），将园的地面压低，其中四面厅则筑于较高的黄石基上，望之宛如置于岛上。园虽无水，而水自在意中。嘉定县秋霞圃后部似亦有此意图，但未及扬州园林明显。我们聪明的匠师能在这种自然条件较为苛刻的情况下，达到中国艺术上"意到笔不到"的意境是难能可贵的。扬州园林中的水面置桥有梁式桥与步石两种。在处理方法上，梁式多数为曲桥，其佳例要推片石山房利用石梁而做的飞梁，古朴浑成，富有山林的气氛；步石则以小盘谷所采用的最为妥帖。一般曲桥总因水位过低，有时转折太僵硬，而缺少自然凌波的感觉，这对园林桥来说，在建造时是应法避免的。片石山房的飞梁形式即弥补了以上缺陷，而另辟蹊径了。

扬州园林素以"叠石胜"，在技术上，过去有很高的评价。因此，今

with windows on four sides sits on a raised yellow-stone foundation as if the architecture sits on an island. Though there is no water in the garden, water is evoked through design. The same design strategy is utilized less effectively at the back of the Qiuxiapu (Garden of the Rosy Clouds of Autumn) in Jiading, Shanghai. It is astonishing that these craftsmen, under harsh natural conditions, could achieve such representational method of Chinese art—"meaning achieved while brushstroke not reached." There are two kinds of bridges built over water in Yangzhou's Gardens: beam bridges and stepping stone bridges. Beam bridges mostly zigzag. Pianshi Shanfang's flying bridge is a great example using a stone as beam; primitive yet simplistic, it perfectly created a scenary of wooded mountain. The bridges in Xiaopangu are the best examples of stepping stone bridges. For these winding bridges, if the water level is too low, the turns are sometimes too stiff, lacking bends and naturalism. For bridges in gardens, it is better to avoid these design flaws during construction. The design of Pianshi Shanfang's bridge using flying bridge invented a new way of making up the design defections.

Gardens in Yangzhou have always excelled in "Piling Rockery" techniques. Most of the existing artificial mountains were made of rocks except the one in Qin's Xiaopangu partly made of soils, and which no longer exits. Since rocks are not produced in Yangzhou, they have to be shipped in from other places and are usually small in size. Mountain peaks are mostly constructed by piecing together small rocks, which are grouped together based on shape, color, vein, texture and quality, and then structurally reinforced with block stones (bricks are also used as structure material, as in the Ming-Dynasty artificial mountain in the Qiao's Garden in Taizhou) and iron fastenings and braces, which are also used for rock embankment around pounds. This method requires significant amounts of labor and maintenance; small rocks tend to fall over time so the peak loses its shape and even the finest example of rockery mountain cannot last long. Still, there are great examples of artificial mountains in Yangzhou, and the ones in Geyuan Garden are the most grand and magnificent among all. The yellow-stone mountain is about nine meters tall, and the Lake Tai stone mountain is about six meters tall. Despite their flaws, these large artificial mountains are still highly accomplished art works. The rockery mountain in Pianshi Shanfang is the most ingenious and imposing among all. The one in Xiaopangu is winding and zigzag, and the one in Yipu is graceful and slender; both are great examples of rockery mountains. The stalactite hanging down in the cave of Diyuan Garden cannot be seen in other

日所存的假山多数以石为主，仅已损毁的秦氏小盘谷似为土石间用。因为扬州不产石，石料运自他地，来料较小。峰峦多用小石包镶，根据石形、石色、石纹、石理、石性等凑合成整体，中以条石（亦有用砖为骨架，早例推泰州乔园明构假山）铁器支挑，加固嵌填后浑然成章，即使水池驳岸亦运用这办法。这样做，人工花费很大，且日久石脱堕地，破坏原形，即有极佳的作品，亦难长久保存。虽然如此，扬州叠山确有其独特的成就，特出的作品以雄伟论，当推个园了。个园的黄石山高约9米，湖石山高约6米，因规模宏大，难免有不够周到的地方，但仍不失为上乘之作。以苍石奇峭论，要算片石山房了，而小盘谷的曲折委婉、逸圃的婀娜多姿皆是佳构。棣园的洞曲中垂钟乳，为扬州园林罕见。其他如寄啸山庄的石壁磴道，亦是较好的例子。在扬州园林的假山中最为突出的是壁岩，其手法的自然逼真，用材的节省，空间的利用，似在苏州之上，实得力于包镶之法。片石山房、小盘谷、寄啸山庄、逸圃、余园等皆有妙作。颇疑此法明末自扬州开始，乾嘉间董道士、戈裕良等人继承了计成、石涛诸人的遗规，并在此基础上得到更大的发展。总之，这些假山在不同程度上达到"异形之山，运不同之石"，体现了石涛所谓"峰与皴合，皴自峰生"的画理，以"高峻雄厚"与苏州的"明秀平远"互相颉颃，南北各抒所长。至于分峰用石及多石并用亦兼补一种石材难以罗致之弊，而以权宜之计另出新腔了。堆叠之法一般皆与苏南相同。其佳者总循"水随山转，山因水活"一原则灵活运用。胶合材料，明代用石灰加细砂和糯米汁，凝结后有时略带红色，常用之于

Yangzhou's gardens. The mountain against the wall and the stone stairway in Jixiao Shanzhuang offer another great example. The artificial mountains leaning against walls are the most outstanding ones among all. With the advanced technique of piecing together small rocks, one uses materials and space wisely, resulting in more natural and realistic mountains than the ones in Suzhou. The examples can be found in Pianshi Shanfang, Xiaopangu, Jixiao Shanzhuang, Yipu, and Yuyuan Garden. I believe this technique was first invented in Yangzhou as early as the late Ming Dynasty, and later during the Qianlong and Jiaqing reigns, Taoist Dong and Ge Yuliang developed the technique inherited from Ji Cheng and Shitao. In summary, these artificial mountains show that different shapes of mountains should be built with different kinds of stones, expressing Shitao's rule of painting that "when the light ink strokes paint the peak, they blended as if the peak generate the strokes." Yangzhou's artificial mountains are steep and solid, standing parallel with Suzhou's artificial mountains, which are flatter yet graceful. The north and the south both have their unique qualities and styles. Regarding using different kinds of stones on different peaks or mixing stones on a single peak, these are strategies to make up the lack of certain kinds of stones. The techniques applied on artificial mountains are more or less similar, in Yangzhou and South Jiangsu. The best examples always apply the principle that "water flows around the mountain; mountain grows out of water." During the Ming, lime, fine sand and sticky rice water were used to hold the stones together. The glue turns red after coagulated and are usually applied on yellow-stone mountains. During the Qing, grass ashes were added to make the glue white, which is suitable for Lake Tai stone mountains like the one in Pianshi Shanfang. A great strategy of caulking is to show the joints while hiding the mortar in between the stones. When applied to yellow stones, the joints appear like natural cracks, emphasizing the ruggedness of stones' surfaces. When applied to Lake Tai stones, the artificial mountain appears as an integrated whole. However, there are rare cases in the whole country achieve such a kind of level.

Regarding walls, existing gardens are centralized in the downtown area and are part of residences, so the enclosing high walls built of finely ground bricks, paired with gate towers of engraved bricks, appear neat and straight. However, the external walls of gardens have all tile-latticed windows and are finished exquisitely. Looked from outside, the Yangzhou gardens are quite different from the gardens in South Jiangsu, which feel like simple and crude. This is due to the fact that owners show off their wealth with their gardens in Yangzhou, but the gardens in South Jiangsu are mostly owned by landed bureaucrats.

黄石山；清代的颜色发白，也有其中加草灰的，适宜用于湖石山。片石山房用的便是后者。好的嵌缝是运用阴嵌的办法，即见缝不见灰，用于黄石山能显出其壁石凹凸多态，仿佛自然裂纹，湖石山采用此法，顿觉浑然一体了。不过，要像这样的水平，其作品在全国范围内也较罕见。

在墙壁的处理上，现存的园林因为多数集中于城区，且是住宅的一部分，所以四周是磨砖砌的高墙，配合了砖刻门楼，外观很是修整平直。不过，园林外墙上都加瓦花窗，墙面做工格外精细，它与苏南园林所给人以简陋的园外感觉不同（苏南园林皆地主官僚所有），是炫富斗财的方法之一。内墙与外墙相同，凡需增加反射效果或需花影月色的地方酌情粉白。园既围以高墙，当然无法眺望园外景色，除在个园中登黄石山可"借景"

城北景物外，余则利用园内的对景来增加园景的变化。寄啸山庄的什锦空窗所构成的景色宛如图画，其住宅与园林部分均利用空窗达到互相"借景"的效果。个园桂花厅前的月门亦起到引人入胜的作用，再从窗棂中所构成的景色，又有移步换影的感觉。在对比手法方面，扬州园林基本与苏南园林相同，多数以建筑物与墙面、山石作对比，运用了开朗、收敛、虚实、高下、远近、深浅、大小、疏密等手法，以小盘谷在这方面运用得最好。寄啸山庄设计亦能从大处着眼，予人以完整醒目的感觉。

扬州园林在建筑方面最显著的特色便是利用楼层，大型园林固然如此，小型的如二分明月楼，也还用了七间的长楼。花厅的体形往往较大，复道的延伸又连续不断，因此虽安排了一些小轩水榭，适与此高大的建筑起了对比作用。这与苏州园林的"婉约轻

Interior walls are similar to exterior walls, which are white-washed in places to add reflection or to display flowers' shadows under moonlight. The gardens are enclosed with high walls, so there is no way to see outside views. In Geyuan Garden, one can climb up the yellow-stone mountain to "borrow views" from the north of the city; other gardens in Yangzhou take advantage of opposite views inside the garden to increase the variations. The sceneries framed by the latticed windows of Jixiao Shanzhuang is just like a picture. The residence and the garden both use latticed windows to borrow views from each other. The views seen through the moon gate in front of the Osmanthus Hall of Geyuan Garden is also fascinating; with the view from the framed windows, visitors are constantly observing different sceneries. Gardens in Yangzhou and in South Jiangsu use similar view contrasting techniques; most buildings are contrasted with wall-surfaces and rockeries, such as open and close, emptiness and solidity, high and low, far and near, deep and shallow, big and small, dense and sparse, and so on. Xiaopangu excels in contrast among all gardens, while Jixiao Shanzhuang offers a wholesome experience by presenting its highlights to the visitors.

The most outstanding characteristic of Yangzhou gardens is the use of storied building, which is apparent in large-scale architecture. Even small-scale gardens like the Erfenmingyue Tower has a seven-bay storied building. Parlors are rather big, and the two-storied walkways extend infinitely, so the small verandas and waterside pavilions are located in contrast with large buildings. Compared to gracefully restrained gardens in Suzhou, such layout in Yangzhou gardens generates the exuberant atmosphere of singing Su Shi's "The Great Yangtze Flows East" accompanied by copper *pipa* and iron clappers. The two-storied walkway of Jixiao Shanzhuang surrounds the garden in a full circle, which is the same in Geyuan Garden when the garden was still complete. Visitors always lose their ways while going up and down in mountains, caves or storied buildings. Suzhou gardens' one-dimensional routes lead visitors through dense willows to bright flowers. The three-dimensional complicatedness of Yangzhou gardens shares the same serendipity. One cannot judge the gardens only based on their architectural plans.

Building structure and buildings details in Yangzhou gardens are combination of southern and northern Chinese styles. A single building's base above ground is built of blue stones in earlier periods and white stones in later periods. Staircases are made of rocks without deliberate arrangement to look natural. Some column bases adopt the northern style in the shape of "ancient mirror" and some are southern style as "stone drum." Columns are quite thick and tall, and the proportion between diameter and height is in between southern and northern styles. Windows are mostly removable windows. Balustrades are also thick and solid. The corner eave is turned up with a small cantilevered

盈"相较，颇有用铜琶铁板唱"大江东去"的气概。寄啸山庄循复道廊可绕园一周，个园盛兴时，情况亦差不多。至于借山登阁，穿洞入穴，上下纵横，游者往往至此迷途，此与苏州园林在平面上的"柳暗花明"境界有异曲同工之妙，不能单以平面略为平整而判其高下。

扬州园林建筑物的外观介于南北之间，而结构与细部的做法亦兼抒两者之长。就单体建筑而论，台基早期用青石，后期用白石，踏跺用天然山石随意点缀，很觉自然。柱础有北方的"古镜"形式，同时也有南方的"石鼓"形式；柱则较为粗挺，其比例又介于南北两者之间。窗多数用和合窗。栏杆亦较肥健。屋角起翘，虽大都用"嫩戗发戗"（由屋角的角梁前端竖立的一根小角梁来起翘），但比苏南来得低平。屋脊则用通花脊，比苏南的厚重。漏窗、地穴（门洞）工细挺拔，图案形式变化多端，轮廓完整，与苏南柔和细腻的感觉不同。门额都用大理石或高资石，而少用砖刻，此又是与苏州显然不同的。建筑的细部手法简洁工整，在线脚与转角的地方略具曲折，虽然总的看来比较直率，但刚中有柔，颇耐寻味。色彩方面，木料皆用本色，外墙不粉白，此固然由于当地气候比较干燥的缘故，但也多少存有以原材精工取胜的意图。其内部梁架皆圆料直材，制作得十分工致完整，间亦有用扁作的。翻轩（建筑物前部的卷棚）尤力求豪华，因为它处于显著的地位，所以格外突出一些。内部以方砖铺地，其间隔有罩与槅扇，材料有紫檀木、红木、楠木、银杏木、黄杨木等，亦有雕漆嵌螺钿与嵌宝玉，或施纱隔。室内家具陈设及屏联的制作同样讲究。海梅（红木）所制的家具与苏、广两地不同，手法和其他艺术一样，富有扬州"雅健"的风格。

corner beam and is lower compared to the ones in South Jiangsu. Roof ridges are decorated with latticed brickwork, thicker and heavier than the ridges in South Jiangsu. Latticed windows and gates in walls are crafted intricately with various patterns and integral structures, which are different from the softer and finer ones in South Jiangsu. Lintels are mostly made of marble or stones from Gaozi, and are rarely made of engraved bricks, which is common in Suzhou. Building details are handled in a neat and clean tradition, with a few twists and turns at wall moldings and corners. Though it looks rather straightforward as a whole, there is gentleness out of the rigidity. Color wise, all the timber retains their original coloring and the exterior walls are not painted white due to the arid climate of Yangzhou. However, the material choice also displays craftsmanship on the raw materials. The interior beams are all round and straight, crafted meticulously, with a few with rectangular cross section. The veranda ceilings (a kind of arched ceiling in front of a building) are designed as luxurious as possible because of the significant location of them. The interior has square bricks as floors, and latticed screens and latticed door leaves as partitions, which are made of red sandalwood, mahogany, *Phoebe nanmu*, gingko, and little-leaf box, or engraved lacquerware inlaid with precious stones or paneled with chiffon. Interior furniture, screens and couplets are also particularly chosen. Mahogany furniture is of an "elegant and invigorating" Yangzhou style, different from the furniture from Suzhou and Guangzhou.

Building typologies are limited in existing Yangzhou gardens, including halls, storied buildings, belvederes, pavilions, pavilions on terrace, land boats, two-storied walkways and winding corridors. The combination of typologies is more regulated compared to gardens in South Jiangsu. The storied building is usually featured prominently at the end of the garden. The hall is usually the centerpiece of the garden. Some storied halls are built at the end of the garden. Land boats and terraced pavilions are built near water. Verandas and belvederes are placed near mountains. Pavilions are either beside the water or on the top of mountains. If the land is limited, then buildings could be built just half (for example, half storied building, half belvedere or half pavilion). Though there are only a few cases, they are adapted to the site and break out of the typology. These unique examples show how rules can be adopted with flexibility. Similar methods are applied to corridors, which are mainly in circuits, and some are built as partition. Forms of corridors include winding ones, stacking and stepping ones, double-lane ones, two-storied ones and so on. According to *Yangzhou Huafang Lu*, there are various types of halls and all are designed carefully: four-sided hall, the halls with flush gable roof, and the storied hall. Buildings' purlin trusses are mostly "turtle shell style"

建筑物在园林中的布置，存今日扬州所有的类型并不多，仅厅堂、楼、阁、亭、榭、舫、复道廊、游廊等，其组合似较苏南园林来得规则。楼常位于园的尽端最突出处，厅往往为一园之主体，有些厅加楼后，形成楼厅就必建在尽端了。其他舫榭临水，轩阁依山。亭有映水与踞山不同的处理。如因地形的限制，则建筑物可做一半，如半楼、半阁、半亭等，虽仅数例，亦发挥了随宜安排的原则，以及同中求异、异中见其规律的灵活善变的应用。廊亦同样不出这些原则与方法，不过以环形路线为主，间有用作分隔的，形式有游廊、叠落廊、复廊、复道廊等。厅堂据《扬州画舫录》所载，名目颇多，处理别出心裁，今日常见的有四面厅、硬山厅、楼厅等，梁架多"回顶鳖壳"式（卷棚式的建筑，在屋顶部仍做成脊）。在材料方面，楠木与柏木厅最为名贵，前者为数尚多，后者今日已少见。园林铺地大部分用鹅子石花街，间有用冰裂纹石。在建筑处理上值得注意的便是内部的曲折多变，其间利用套房、楼、廊、小院、假山、石室等的组合造成"迷境"的感觉。现存的逸圃，尚能见到，此亦扬州园林重要特征之一。

花木的栽植是园林中重要的组织部分，各地花木有其地方特色，因此反映在园林中亦有不同的风格。扬州花木因风土地理的关系，同一品种，其姿态容颜也与南北两地有异。一般说来，枝干花朵比较硕秀。在树木的配置上，以松、柏、栝、榆、枫、槐、银杏、女贞、梧桐、黄杨等为习见。苏南后期园林中杨柳几乎绝迹，然则在扬州园林中却常能见到，且更具有强烈的地方色彩。因为此地的杨柳在外形上高劲，枝条疏修，颇多画意，下部的体形也不大，植于园中没有不调和的感觉。梧桐在扬州生长甚速，碧干笼荫，不论在园林或庭院中，都

(round ridge roof). Material wise, halls built of *Phoebe nanmu* and cypress are the most precious among all. There are still plenty ones of *Phoebe nanmu*, but the ones with cypress are rarely seen. Garden grounds are mostly paved in patterns with pebbles, and sometimes with stones of cracked-ice pattern. A noticeable architectural feature is the intricate interior space, using combinations of suites, storied buildings, corridors, small yards, artificial mountains and stone chambers to created mysterious spatial feeling. This important feature of Yangzhou gardens can still be found in Yipu.

Horticulture is also a very important part of landscape architecture. Flowers and trees from different areas have their local traits, reflecting different styles in gardens. Because of weather and geography, the same species of flowers and trees in Yangzhou look different from ones planted in the north or the south. In general, Yangzhou's plants and flowers are larger and more vigorous. Common tree types include pine, cypress, juniper, elm, maple, pagoda, gingko, broad-leaf privet, Chinese parasol, little-leaf box and so on. During later periods, weeping willows are rare in gardens in South Jiangsu, but very common in Yangzhou gardens. Weeping willows in Yangzhou have strong local characteristics: strong and sturdy, twigs thick and scattered, quite picturesque. The base of the trees is not too big, and blends harmoniously with the garden. Chinese parasol trees grow quite fast in Yangzhou with their green trunks and dense canopies. Whether planted in gardens or courtyards, Chinese parasol trees create pleasant, cooling shades. Together with weeping willows, they dominate the city's significant scenery in spring and summer time. Flowering trees include sweet osmanthus, crabapple, Yulan magnolia, camellia, pomegranate, wisteria, crape myrtle, plum, wintersweet, flowering peach, banksia rose, rose bush, China rose, azalea and so on. In front of a hall or a veranda, sweet osmanthus, crabapple, Yulan magnolia and crape myrtle are planted. Other trees such as maples or elms are planted where they are needed. In Yangzhou gardens, arbors were planted to provide cooling shades whereas flowering trees were for observation, and their contours, color and fragrance are the most important standards. Pines and cypresses are planted to highlight a rockery mountain's rugged and worn feature. A few weeping willows are placed near water. Plantain, bamboo and nandina add a picturesque touch decorating small yards or large gardens, planted in the corner of a wall or walkway, under the eaves, alongside wintersweet or chrysanthemum. The "book-binder grass" (*Ophiopogon japonicus*) look green in all four seasons, no matter planted beside a mountain, tree, stairway, or road, and the grass looks like white balls during winter when covered by snow. Along with begonia in stone crevices, they are irreplaceable decorations in gardens. The grass is also used to improve a rockery mountain's appearance or to cover its drawbacks, similar to adding moss in landscape

给人以清雅凉爽之感，与柳色各占春夏二季的风光。花树有桂、海棠、玉兰、山茶、石榴、紫藤、紫薇、梅、腊梅、碧桃、木香、蔷薇、月季、杜鹃等。在厅轩堂前，多用桂、海棠、玉兰、紫薇诸品，其他如亭畔、榭旁的枫榆等则因地位的需要而栽植。乔木与花树同建筑的关系，在扬州园林中，前者作为遮阴之用，后者用作观赏之需，姿态与色香仍是选择的最重要标准。在假山间，为了衬托山容苍古，酌植松柏；水边配置少许垂杨；至于芭蕉、竹、天竹等，不论用来点缀小院，补白大园，或在曲廊转处、墙阴檐角，或与腊梅、丛菊等组合，都能入画；书带草不论在山石边、树木根旁，以及阶前路旁，均给人以四季常青的好感。冬季初雪匀披，粉白若球，书带草与石隙中的秋海棠都是园林绿化中不可缺少的小点缀。至于以书带草增假山生趣或掩饰假山堆叠的疵病处，真有山水画中点苔的妙处。芍药、牡丹更是家栽户植。《芍药谱》[8]载："扬州芍药，名于天下，非特以多为夸也。其敷腴盛大而纤丽巧密，皆他州所不及。"李白诗（《送孟浩然之广陵》）："烟花三月下扬州。"可以想见其盛况。因此，花坛药栏便在园林中占有显著的地位，其形式有以假山石叠的自然式，有用砖与白石砌的图案式，形状很多，皆匠心独运。春时繁花似锦，风光宛如洛城。树木的配合仍运用了孤植与群植的两种基本方法；群植中有用同一品种的，亦有用混合的树群布置，主要的还是从园林的大小与造景的意图出发。如小园，宜孤植，但树的姿态须加选择；大园多群植，亦须注意假山的形态、地形的高低大小，做到有分有合，有密有疏。若假山不高，主要山顶便不可植树，为了衬托出山势的苍郁与高峻，非植于山阴略低之处不可，使峰出树梢之间，自然饶有山林之意了。此理不独植树如此，

paintings. Herbaceous and arboreous peony are favorites, planted in every household. According to *Shaoyao Pu* (*Collection of Herbaceous Peony*)[8], "The herbaceous peony of Yangzhou is famous worldwide. It is not only praised for its abundance. The flower is full, beautiful and delicate, better than the ones from other places." Li Bai also writes about the herbaceous peony; one can picture the magnificent scenery in *Song Meng Haoran Zhi Guangling* (*Seeing Meng Haoran off to Yangzhou*), "He rides to Yangzhou in March, surrounded by flowers." Therefore, peony beds and nurseries are important in gardens. There are various types and shapes designed ingeniously, including natural shape of rockeries, or built with bricks and white stones. In spring, beds and nurseries are filled with peony flowers, and the whole city is as vigorous as Luoyang, home of arboreous peonies. The planting of trees is based on two basic strategies: individually or in groups, mainly based on the garden size and the design intent. Small gardens are more suitable with individual trees but the trees' postures should be picked carefully. Large gardens mostly have trees in groups to match rockery contours and the elevation and size of the terrain to avoid stiffness. If the artificial mountain is short, there should be no trees on the peak. In order to emphasize the mountain's color and height, trees must be planted low, at the mountain's shady side, so that the peak is higher than the top of the tree. Then, the garden will feel like a forest. The strategies mentioned here not only apply to tree planting, but also on the building of pavilions. The relationship between pavilions, trees and mountains must be considered in heights and distances. Planting a pine tree lying on water at the foot of a mountain is a great way of organizing the composition of the scenery. It is the same with wisteria hanging from the mountain and lotus flowers growing from the water surface, but the number of the plants must be controlled to present a clear design intention and view. Trees should be planted based on their adaptability to bright and dark sides; for example, camellia, sweet osmanthus, pines and cypresses are suitable to grow in shady places, while bamboos can add vitality to the corners of gardens.

Different from Suzhou and Hangzhou, Yangzhou's artistic potted plants and miniature landscapes are strong, sturdy and weather-beaten. Local horticulturists are adept at cutting and bundling; over a long period of time, they can train trees into shapes of "knots," "cloud sheets" or "bends." Pine, cypress, little-leaf box, chrysanthemum, camellia, azalea, plum, bitter orange flower, jasmine, kumquat, orchid and Hui orchid are all great options for potted plants, either growing in earth or water. Sweet flags that grow purely out of water, in bowls out of palm sheaths, and stay green all year round, and the potted asters cultivated by floriculturists, are both unique to Yangzhou. These plants are great

建亭亦然，而亭与树与山的关系，必高下远近得宜才是。山麓的水边有用横线条的卧松临水，亦不失为求得画面统一的好办法。山间垂藤萝，水面点荷花，亦皆以少出之，使意到景生即可。至于园内因日照关系有阴阳面的不同，在考虑种树时应加注意其适应性，如山茶、桂、松、柏等皆宜植阴处，补竹则处处均能增加生意。

扬州盆景刚劲坚挺，能耐风霜，与苏杭不同。园艺家的剪扎工夫甚深，称之为"疙瘩""云片"及"弯"等，都是说明剪扎所成的各种姿态的特征，这些都是非短期内可以培养成的。松、柏、黄杨、菊花、山茶、杜鹃、梅、玐玐、茉莉、金橘、兰、蕙等都是盆景的好主题。又有山水盆景，分旱盆、水盆两种，咫尺山林，亦多别出心裁。棕碗菖蒲，根不着土，以水滋养，终年青葱，为他处所不常见，它如艺菊，扬州花匠师对此有独到之技。以这些来点缀园林，当然锦上添花了。园林山石间，因乔木森严，不宜栽花，就要运用盆景来点缀，这种办法从宋代起即运用了，不但地面如此，即池中的荷花，亦莫不用盆荷入池的。因此，谈中国园林的绿化，不能不考虑盆景。

按扬州画派的作品，以花卉为多，摹写对象当然为习见的园林花木，经画家们的挥洒点染，都成了佳作，则扬州园林中的花木其影响可见。反之，画家对园林花木批红判白，以及剪裁、配置、构图等对花木匠师亦有一定的启发与促进。扬州产金鱼，天然禽鸟兼有南北品种，且善培养笼鸟，这些对园林都有所增色。

总之，造园有法而无式，变化万千，新意层出。园因景胜，景因园异，其妙处在于"因地制宜"与相互"借景"（"妙在因借"），做到得体（"精在体宜"），始能别具一格。扬州园

decoration to gardens, improving sceneries. Mountains are usually shaded by arbors, where flowers rarely survive, so potted plants are adopted to decorate instead. This strategy was already undertaken as early as the Song. Most lotuses growing in ponds are potted. Therefore, when discussing Chinese landscape planting, potted plants cannot be ignored.

Flowers are themes most commenly seen in the works of Yangzhou school of traditional Chinese paintings. Yangzhou painters portrayed plants and flowers from the gardens and created masterpieces, in which one can see the huge influences of these subjects. At the same time, the way these plants and flowers are chosen, arranged and composed by the painters inspired local horticulturists to improve. Yangzhou is home to goldfish and birds, and locals also breed caged birds. All these contributed to the gardens in Yangzhou.

In general, there are standards for gardening, but no set formulas. No garden is the same as another, and new ideas develop on old ones. Gardens stand out with their sceneries and sceneries change from one garden to another. A garden's success lies in its adaptability to the site and its borrowing of views from its surroundings. A garden can only be distinctive if it does everything to the correct extent. Yangzhou gardens accommodate characteristics of both southern and northern gardens and are a school of their own. The gardens contain gracefulness within their imposing forms. As described in literature, "Strong brush writes tender feelings." Buildings are tall and spacious. Artificial mountains are rich and aged. Latticed walls are perforated and exquisite. Vibrant trees and gorgeous flowers are grown in natural environments and bred by local gardeners afterwards. All these elements in Yangzhou gardens are incomparable to anywhere else. The artificial mountains are piled up using various kinds of stones, using the strategy of piecing together numerous small stones. Peaks of the mountains are made up of different stones. Dry gardens have the illusion of water. All these design strategies, from using a variety of materials to adapting gardens to their sites, greatly influence garden design today. However, some of the ponds in Yangzhou gardens are dull and water fails to permeate the gardens; in the past, rockery mountains and buildings would have been in harmony to achieve the gardens' sublimity. Ordinary courtyards also have flowers and bamboos planted. Abors provide shades, in company with flowering trees, wisteria, potted plants or small rocks, to form miniature landscapes. Gardens and these elements enriched city dwellers' cultural life and altogether enlarged Yangzhou's greenery coverage. This great tradition is kept alive today.

林综合了南北的特色，自成一格，雄伟中寓明秀，得雅健之致，借用文学上的一句话来说，真所谓"健笔写柔情"了。而堂庑廊亭的高敞挺拔、假山的沉厚苍古、花墙的玲珑透漏，更是别处所不及。至于树木的硕秀、花草的华滋，则受自然条件的影响，且经匠师们的加工而形成。假山的堆叠广泛地应用了多种石类，以小石拼镶的技术，以及分峰用石、旱园水做等因材致用、因地制宜的手法，对今日造园都有一定的借鉴作用。唯若干水池似少变化，未能发挥水在园林中的弥漫之意，似少构成与山石建筑物等相互成趣的高度境界。一般庭院中，亦能栽花种竹，荫以乔木，配合花树，或架紫藤，罗置盆景片石，安排一些小景。这些都丰富了当时城市居民的文化生活，同时集腋成裘，又扩大了城市绿化的面积，是当地至今还延续的一种传统。

## 卢宅（180—181 页）

卢宅在康山街。清光绪间盐商江西卢绍绪所建，造价为纹银七万两，是今存扬州最大的住宅建筑。大门用水磨砖刻门楼，配以大照壁。入门北向为倒座（与南向正屋相对的房屋），经二门有厅二进，皆面阔七间，以当中三间为主厅，其旁两间为会客读书之处，内部用罩（用木制漏空花纹做成的分隔）及槅扇（落地长窗）间隔。院中以大漏窗与两旁的小院区分。小院中置湖石花台，配以树木，形成幽静的空间，与中部畅达的大厅不同。再入为楼厅二进，面阔亦七间，系主人居住之处。厅后二进，面阔易为五间，系亲友临时留居的地方。东为厨房，今毁。宅后有园名"意园"。池在园东北，濒池建书斋及藏书楼二进，自成一区。池东原有旱船，今亦废。园南依墙建盔顶亭，有游廊导向北部。余地栽植乔木，以桂为主。此宅用材精选湖广杉木，皆不髹饰。装修皆用

### Lu's Residence (Page 180-181)

Lu's residence sits at Kangshan Street. It was built by a salt merchant from Jiangxi province, Lu Shaoxu, during the Guangxu reign of the Qing Dynasty. The construction sum was seventy thousand taels of silver. It is the largest extant residential building in Yangzhou. Its front gate is made of finely ground bricks with carvings and decorated with a giant screen wall. Behind the gate there sits a converse room (the room opposite the south facing main suite). Passing the second gate, there are two rows of buildings each with a seven-bay hall. The three bays in the center are used as a central room, and the other two on both sides are for reception and reading purposes. The interior is segmented by latticed wooden screens and lang latticed door leaves. The central courtyard is separated from side ones with large latticed windows. Side courtyards are quite different from the spacious central hall. Flowerbeds made of Lake Tai stones and trees are planted to create serene spaces in the courtyards. In the north, there are two rows of seven-bay halls that serve as the owner's residence. Furthermore, there are two more rows of five-bay buildings behind the wall, serving as temporary guest quarters. East side, there is kitchen that no longer exists. Behind the residence, there is a garden named Yiyuan. The pond is at the northeast of the garden, near which there is an independent zone of two rows of buildings including a study and a library. Originally, there was a land boat at the east side of the pond. Against the garden's southern wall, there sits a pavilion with a helmet-shaped rooftop, from which a corridor leads to the north. Arbors, mainly sweet osmanthus trees, are planted covering the rest of the garden. The residence's building material is mainly fir wood from the Hunan and Hubei provinces, all of which unpainted. The interior material uses delicately-carved *Phoebe nanmu*. Though the residence was constructed in the late period of Chinese feudalism, the architecture is tall and spacious—a classic representative of luxury houses.

### Wangshi Xiaoyuan (Page 182-183)

Wangshi Xiaoyuan (Wang's Small Garden, salt merchant Wang Boping's residence) sits at Diguandi. Expanded during the Republican years, it is the most complete large residence in Yangzhou, which is made up of three sequences of buildings—each with three rows. The eastern and western parlors are decorated in different fashions. The entrance to the eastern parlor is a gate of unadorned woven bamboo strips—simple and classic. The parlor is built of cypress and is devided into front and back with latticed screens and latticed door leaves embedded with exquisite marble divide the space into front and back. To the south of the parlor, there is a three-bay converse building. In the courtyard, there is a flowerbed of Lake Tai stone. Winter sweets and macrocephalus are planted in it. A door on the east opens onto a tiny piece of land, which expands the space. The western parlor is separated from the courtyard by a gate. Inside the courtyard, there is an artificial mountain. To the east, there is a boat-shaped veranda, with a veranda linked to it and a pool at its foot. A brick platform is built under the veranda, where potted plants can be placed, to form interesting reflection in the water. Walking inside the parlor, and looking into the courtyard

楠木，雕刻工细。虽建筑年代较迟，然屋宇高敞，规模宏大，是后期盐商所建豪华住宅的代表。

## 汪氏小苑（182—183 页）

汪氏小苑（盐商汪伯屏宅）在地官第，民国间扩建，为今存扬州大住宅中最完整的一处。它分三路，各三进。东西花厅布置各别。东花厅入口用竹丝门，甚古朴。厅用柏木建造，内部置罩及槅扇，槅扇上嵌大理石，皆雕刻精工，作前后分隔之用，其南有倒座三间。院中置湖石花台，栽腊梅、琼花。东有门，入内仅一小小余地，所谓"明有实无"，以达扩大空间的目的。西花厅以月门与小院相隔，院内中有假山一丘，面东置船轩，辍以游廊，下凿小池，轩下砌砖台，可置盆景，映水成趣。自厅中穿月门以望院中，花木扶疏，山石参差，宛如图画。宅北后园列东西两部，间以花墙月门。西部北建花厅六间，用罩分隔为二。厅西有书斋三间，缀五色玻璃，其前有廊横陈。两者之间，植紫薇二株，亭亭如盖，依稀掩映，内外相望有不尽之意。厅南叠假山，为牡丹台，东部亦筑花台，似甚平淡，两部运用花墙间隔，人们的视线穿过漏窗月门望隔园景色，深幽清灵，发挥了很大的"借景"作用。此处当以住宅建筑占主要部分，而园则相辅而已，因面积不大，所以题为"小苑春深"。

## 赵宅（184—185 页）

赞化宫赵宅（布商赵海山宅），厅堂三进，南向。门屋及厨房等附属建筑皆建于墙外，花园亦与住宅以高墙隔离，但亦可由门屋直接入园，避免与住宅相互干扰，在建筑平面的分隔上来说，很是明晰。花园前部东向有书斋三间，以曲廊与后部分隔，后有宽敞的花厅两进，与住宅的规模很相称。

through the moon gate, one sees a picturesque scenery of well-planted flowers and trees, along with rugged rockeries. The backyard to the north of the residence is devided into an eastern and western section by a moon gate and a latticed wall. The northwestern section has a six-bay parlor to the north, divided into two parts by a latticed screen. To the west of the parlor, there is a three-bay study decorated with colored glass. A corridor sits in front of the study; in between the corridor and the study, there are two crape myrtles which form a canopy to shield the space from sunlight. Views from both the inside and outside seem to go on forever. To the south of the parlor, rocks are piled up to form a peony flowerbed. The flowerbed in the eastern section is comparably boring. The western and eastern sections are segmented with latticed windows. When people look through latticed windows and the moon gate to see the other parts, the sceneries are serene and quiet thanks to view borrowing. This place is dominated by residential buildings, and the garden is only a supplement. Due to the garden's small size, it is called "Xiaoyuan Chunshen" (A Small Garden With Deep Spring).

### Zhao's Residence (Page 184-185)

Zhao's residence at Zanhuagong, owned by cloth merchant Zhao Haishan, has three rows of halls facing south. The portal, kitchen and other affiliated buildings are constructed outside of the wall. The garden is also separated from the residence by tall walls, but visitors can still enter the garden directly through the portal to avoid mutual disturbance between the residential and garden sections. Segmentation on the architectural plan is clear. In front of the garden, facing east, there is a three-bay study separated from the back by a winding corridor. A spacious two-row parlor sits behind the garden, matching the impressive scale of the residence.

### Wei's Residence (Page 186-187)

Wei's residence, owned by the salt merchant Wei Cigeng, is on Yongsheng Street. It is a medium scale residence with a west-facing front gate. The building sits on an irregular plan, but with a clear hierarchy. Dwellings are on the rectangular eastern section and the garden is on the irregular western section. There are four rows of residential buildings, including the converse rooms, and each row has five bays. The hall in the center has three bays, with a suite of rooms on either side, and a small yard for residential living. This style of suites is connected to the living rooms, but also independent from each other. Yards have efficient ventilation and sunlight and are effective in expanding both interior and exterior spaces. The garden's front is narrow and the back is wide. In the front and close to the front gate, there is a storage room. The back of the garden is divided into two zones. In the front zone, there is a four-sided hall called "Chuitai" ( Flute Terrace). Its lintel is inscribed with the following line in Zheng Banqiao's calligraphy: "Songs and Flutes about Ancient Yangzhou." The hall is companied by rockery mountains, Yulan magnolias, Chinese parasol trees and a small belvedere at the southeast corner. The back zone serves as a contrast for the front and again is divided into western and eastern sections. In the eastern section, there is a land boat beside a small belvedere and a yellow-stone mountain at the foot of a latticed wall, with nandinas and little-leaf boxes planted. Seen

## 魏宅（186—187 页）

魏宅（盐商魏次庚宅）在永胜街，属中型住宅，大门西向，总体为不规则的平面。因此，将东首划出长方形的地带作为住宅，西首不规则的余地辟为园林，主次很是鲜明。住宅连倒座计四进，皆面阔五间。它的布置特点：厅为三间带两厢，旁皆配套房小院，在当时作为居住之用。这类套房处理得很是恰当，它与起居部分实联而似分，互不干扰，尤其小院不论在采光通风与扩大室内外空间上皆得到较好效果。园前狭后宽，前部邻大门处有杂屋，后部划分作前后两区。前区筑四面厅名"吹台"，郑板桥书额为"歌吹古扬州"，配以山石、玉兰、青桐，面对东南角建有小阁。后区为前区的陪衬，又东西划为两部分。东部置旱船，旁辅小阁，花墙下叠黄石山、栽天竹、黄杨，穿花墙外望，景色隐约。这园虽小，而置两大建筑物，尚能宽绰有余，是利用花墙划分得宜，互相得以因借之法，使空间层次增加，也是宅旁余地设计的一种方法。

## 刘宅（188页）

仁丰里刘宅，宅不大，门东向，入内沿门屋筑西向屋一排，前有高墙。天井作狭长形，可避夏季炎阳与冬季烈风，而夏季因墙高地狭，门牖爽通，反觉受风较多。墙内南向厅三进，而末进除置套房外，更增密室（套房内的套房）。厅旁有花墙，过月门，内有花厅，置山石花木。整个建筑设计是灵活运用东向基地的一个例子。

## 贾宅（189页）

大武城巷贾宅，清光绪间盐商贾颂平所有，大门东向。厅计两路，皆南向而建，而东部诸厅设计尤妙，每一厅皆有庭院，有栽花植竹为花坛，有凿池叠石为小景，再环以游廊，映以疏棂，多清新之意。宅西偏原有园林，今废。

through latticed walls, exterior views are indistinct. The garden is small, but spacious enough for two large buildings, because of the latticed walls in the garden, which appropriately divide the garden into zones and borrow views from each other to create layered views. This is design strategy for empty spaces beside the residence.

### Liu's Residence (Page 188)

Liu's residence at Renfeng Li is not a huge one. Stepping into the east facing entrance, there is a row of rooms facing west. In the front, there is a tall wall, and a narrow rectangular yard keeps the building free from the sun in summer and the wind in winter. In the summer, because of the tall wall, narrow yard, wide open windows and doors, there is plenty of summer breeze. Behind the wall, there are three rows of halls facing south, and a secret room is hidden in the suite of rooms in the last row. A latticed wall sits beside the hall, and through a moon gate, there is a parlor with flowers, trees and rockery mountains. Liu's residence is a good example in strategically dealing with an east facing site.

### Jia's Residence (Page 189)

Jia's residence at Dawucheng Xiang was owned by the salt merchant Jia Songping in the Guangxu reign of the Qing Dynasty. The front entrance faces the east, and two sequences of halls faces the south. The halls in the east are all meticulously designed and every hall has a courtyard. Some courtyards have parterres planted with flowers and bamboos, and some have a pond and rocks that compose a small scenery. The courtyards are encircled with a corridor, and latticed windows are carved in the walls, evoking fresh and cool feelings. There was a garden to the west of the residence that no longer exists today.

**Xinyuan Garden (Page 190)**

Xinyuan Garden at Renfeng Li was owned by Zhou Yifu. The entrance faces the west. Inside the gate, there is a row of rooms facing west, which is a common strategy for sites facing east in Yangzhou. A courtyard is enclosed by the hall facing south, the eastern and western corridors, and a converse room. A parlor sits at the west of the hall. There is a half pavilion at the entrance of the parlor, and a study room at the opposite. The space south of the hall is seperated by latticed walls, and some empty spaces about a foot away make up imaginary scenery. An aged sweet osmanthus tree extends over the latticed walls. When autumn comes, the courtyard is immersed in the tree's fragrance, and visitors inside the courtyard feel that the courtyard is filled with heavenly aroma. (Sweet osmanthus tree must be surrounded with walls so that its fragrance does not escape.) Behind the hall, a moon gate opens to the west; its lintel is inscribed with the name of the garden "Xinyuan." Inside the garden, there is a fish pond, a zigzag bridge and a small pavilion. The parlor is decorated with gingko wood, and the unpainted material makes the interior more elegant and fresh. The floor in front of the hall is paved with white stones in a very clean and level manner. The residential area is quite small, and more space is devoted to greenery. There are relatively more changes on the original plan, developed by previous owners during expansion.

## 辛园（190 页）

仁丰里辛园，为周挹扶宅，大门东向，入内筑西向房屋一排，为扬州东向基地的惯用手法。南向的厅与东西两廊及倒座构成四合院。厅西花厅入口处建一半亭，对面为书斋，厅南以花墙间隔，其外尺余空地留作虚景。老桂树超出花墙之上，秋时满院飘香，人临其境，便体会到一种天香院落的境界（桂树必周以墙，香不散）。厅后西通月门，有额名"辛园"。园内中凿鱼池，有曲桥，旁建小亭。花厅装修以银杏木本色制成，未髹漆，更是雅洁。厅前以白石拼合铺地，很是平整。此宅居住部分小，绿化范围大，平面上的变化比较多，是过去宅主在历次扩建中逐步形成的现象。

## 黄氏汉庐（191 页）

石牌楼黄氏汉庐，清道光年间为金石书画家吴熙载的故居。大门北向，入门有院，其西首的"火巷"可达南向的四合院。院以正屋与倒座相对而建，院子作横长形，石板墁地。此为北向住宅的一例。

## 匏庐（192—193 页）

　　甘泉路匏庐，民国初年资本家卢殿虎建。门东向，入内南向筑大厅，其南端为花厅，厅北以黄石叠花坛，厅南以湖石叠山，殊葱郁。山右构水轩，蕉影拂窗，明静映波。园极西，穿角门，北端又有黄石一丘，越门可绕至厅后。宅的东部有一片曲尺形地，以游廊花墙通贯。小池东南隅筑方亭，隔池尽端筑小轩三间，皆随廊可达，面积虽小，尚觉委婉紧凑。此宅是利用东门南向以及利用不规则余地进行设计的一例。

Huangshi Hanlu at Shipailou was the residence of calligraphist Wu Xizai during the Daoguang reign of the Qing Dynasty. The gate faces north and opens into a courtyard. The fire lane at the west end of the courtyard leads to another courtyard. The main house in the courtyard faces south, sitting opposite the converse rooms. The courtyard is rectangular and paved with stone slabs. This is an example of north-facing residences.

### Paolu (Page 192-193)

Paolu on Ganquan Road was built by the capitalist Lu Dianhu during early Republican years. Inside the east-facing entrance, there sits a main hall facing south, whose southern end is a parlor. A parterre made of yellow stones is at north of the parlor. An artificial mountain of Lake Tai stones sits at the south of the parlor, surrounded by greenery. To the right of the mountain, there is a veranda constructed beside the pond. The swaying shadows of plantains are casted upon its windows, and the veranda is reflected in the clear pond. Beyond the west gate, there is another yellow-stone artificial mountain at the northern tip. Visitors could see the back of the parlor through another gate. In the east of the residence, there is a piece of land in the form of a carpenter's square, connected by a winding corridor and latticed walls. A square pavilion is located at the southeastern corner of the small pond. A three-bay veranda is built across the pond, which is accessible by the corridor. Though the veranda is small, it still feels elegant and compact. This residence is an example of a south facing main hall and a eastern gate on an irregular site.

### Residential Compound at Dingjiawan (Page 194)

The residential compound at Dingjiawan had two residences in the same gateway—one in the east and one in the west. The east one has a three-sided courtyard, which is divided into front and back sections by latticed walls, and all the buildings are spacious and flexible enough to cover two bays. The west one has two successive three-sided courtyards, each with three-bay rooms aligned in a different way. This type of residence has the advantage of adapting to specific sites and freely dividing spaces.

### No. 2 Niubeijing

No. 2 Niubeijing is one of the smallest residences. It faces south and there is only a three-bay hall behind the gate. The coutyard is made up of the hall, two wing rooms and a converse room. The kitchen is attached outside the coutyard. This kind of layout is the most basic unit of residences in Yangzhou.

## 丁家湾某宅（194 页）

丁家湾某宅，扬州住宅中用总门的代表性一例。总门内东西各有两宅：东宅有三合院，天井中以花墙分隔，形成前后两部分，而房屋面阔皆作两间，处理很灵活；西宅正屋二进皆三合院，面阔三间，二进的三合院排列又非一致。此类住宅有因地制宜、分隔自由的好处。

## 牛背井二号某宅

牛背井二号某宅，最小住宅的一例。南向，入门仅厅三间，由厢房、倒座构成一个四合院，外附厨房。这种平面布局是扬州住宅的基本单元。

扬州城由平行的新旧两城组合成今日的城区。运河绕城，小秦淮自北门流入，为新旧两城的分界。旧城南北又以汶河贯串，所以河道都是南北平行的。由于河道平直，道路及建筑物可以得到较规则的布局。其间主要干道为通东西南北的十字大街，与大街垂直的便是坊巷，这一点在旧城更为突出。巷名称"头巷""二巷"……"九巷"，和北京的"头条胡同""二条胡同"……相似。新城因后期富商官僚的大住宅与若干商业建筑的发展，布局比旧城零乱，颇受江南城市风格的影响。新城的湾子街就不是垂直线，好像北京的斜街，是一条交通捷径。在这许多街道中掺杂了不少小巷，有的还是"死胡同"，因此看来似乎复杂，其实仍旧井然有序，脉络自存。过去大的巷口还建有拱门，当地称为"圈门"，它是南北街坊布置的介体，兼有南北城市街坊布置的特征。

住宅按街巷的朝向布置，在处理上大体符合"因地制宜"的要求，较

Today's Yangzhou is made of two parallel cities—one old and one new. The canal surrounds the city and Xiaoqinhuai River flows into the city from the north gate, separating the new and the old parts of the city. The old town is again connected by Wenhe River from the north to the south, so all the riverways are parallel in the north-south direction. Since the riverways are rather straight, roads and buildings are laid out in a regular manner. The city's main road is the cross streets connecting north-south and east-west, and lanes are perpendicular to the main road, which is featured prominently in the old town. Lanes are named as Tou Xiang (Main Lane), Er Xiang (Second Lane)...Jiu Xiang (Ninth Lane), similar to Hutongs in Beijing such as Toutiao Hutong (Main Hutong), Ertiao Hutong (Second Hutong). The new town is less organized than the old town as it was dominated by rich merchants and officials' huge residences and developments of several pieces of commercial architecture, influenced by urban styles of cities in the Jiangnan area. The Wanzi Street in the New City is not straight. Just like the Xie Street (Diagonal Street) in Beijing, it serves as a traffic shortcut. A lot of small lanes mingle with the main street, some among which are "sihutong" (dead-end). The road system might seem a bit complicated; however, it is still well organized with clear rules. Before, major lanes had arches, which are called "quanmen" (circle gates). These arches serve as features for lanes, and they are characteristics of urban layouts of cities in both the south and the north.

Residences are laid out based on the orientation of streets and lanes, which mostly meet the requirements of adaptation to the site. Their locations in the city are rather flexible, while their interior layouts are intricate with plenty of variations. Residences are usually located on east-west lanes, so they can directly face the south, or, if the entrance faces the north, the main buildings can still face the south. There are also some residences in north-south lanes; in order to have a true south orientation, some of them were designed to face the south despite their east or west entrances. Several medium and small-sized residences are combined with the same entrance, so they look very organized from the exterior though there are plenty of variations in the interior. This is a great strategy of using a main gate to hide small buildings inside larger ones and gather smaller parts into a whole. During feudal society, this strategy satisfied both the needs for the whole clan to live together and the security requirement for feudal families. The method also helped the city of Yangzhou to have an overall clean and tidy appearance.

Nowadays, most of the residences preserved in Yangzhou are large and medium sized. These residences usually have gardens and courtyards of different sizes. Residential spaces thus include plenty of greenery to make up a comfortable living environment.

Layouts of the residences are usually in the style of a courtyard, with a three-bay hall as the main block; some halls are as wide as five-bays. Just as in *Gongduan Yingzao Lu*, "If the hall has five bays then the wing rooms should have latticed door leaves or latticed screens, so that three bays are brighter and two bays are darker." There also

为灵活，而内部尤曲折多变。住宅主要位于通东西的坊巷中，因此都能取得正南的朝向，或北门南向。通南北的坊巷中，亦有些住宅，因为要利用正南或偏南的朝向，于是产生了东门南向或西门南向的住宅。又运用总门的办法，将若干中小型不同平面的住宅，利用一个总门，非常灵活地组合成一个整体——这样，在坊巷中，它的外貌仍旧十分整齐，而内部却有许多变化，这是大中藏小、化零为整的巧办法。在封建社会，这不但能满足聚族而居的生活方式和封建家庭的治安防卫需要，并且在市容整齐等方面也相应地带来了一定的好处。

扬州城区今日尚存的多为大中型住宅，这些住宅的特点都配合着大小不等的园林和庭院，使居住区中包括了充裕的绿化地带，形成了安适的居住环境。

住宅平面一般采用院落式，以面阔三间的厅堂为主体，更有面阔到五间的，即《工段营造录》所谓："如五间则两梢间设樀子或飞罩，今谓明三暗五。"也有四间、两间的，皆按地基面积而定。虽然也有面阔七间的，其实仍以三间为主，左右各加两间客厅，如康山街卢宅的厅堂。大中型住宅旁设弄名"火巷"，是女眷、仆从出入之处。如大型住宅有两路以上的"火巷"，又为宅内主要交通道。扬州的"火巷"比苏州"避弄"（俗称"备弄"，今据明代文震亨著《长物志》卷一）开朗修直，给居住者以明洁坦直的感觉，尤其以紫气东来巷龚姓沧州别墅的"火巷"最为广阔，当时可乘轿出入。厅堂除一进不连庑的"老人头"外，尚有两面连庑的"曲尺房"（由两面建筑物相连，平面形成曲尺形）、三面连庑的"三间两厢"（厅堂左右加厢的三合院）以及"四合头"（四合院）、"对合头"（两厅相对，又称对照厅）等。以"三间两厢"及"四合头"作走马楼的称"串楼"。厅堂的排列顺序：前为大厅，后为内厅（女

exist four-bay and two-bay buildings, and the size depends on the area of the sites. Seven-bay halls mainly have the three bays in the center, and two living rooms are added to both wings, like the hall in Lu's residence on Kangshan Street. A side lane called "huoxiang" (fire lane) is usually attached to a large or medium sized residence, serving as the entrance for women and servants. If a large residence has more than two fire lanes, then they are also major traffic roads inside the residence. Yangzhou's "huoxiang" is straighter and more open than Suzhou's "bilong" (also called "beilong"). Today, we use the former, as in vol.1 of *Changwu Zhi* (*Records of Non-Essentials* written by Wen Zhenheng in the Ming Dynasty). The fire lane part of Cangzhou Villa of the Gong Family at Ziqidonglai Xiang was wide enough for sedan chairs to pass through. There are five types of halls. The first type is called "Old Man's Head." This type of hall is a single row deep with no wing rooms. The second type is "Carpenter's Square Shape"—both sides of the hall are attached to a wing room. The third type, "Three Bays Two Wings," refers to a three-bay hall with wing rooms on both sides to form a three-sided courtyard. The fourth type is "Four Compound," which is a quadrangle courtyard made up of a hall, a converse room and wing rooms on both ends. The fifth type is called "Opposite Compound" with two halls facing each other in opposite directions. If "Three Bays Two Wings" and "Four Compound" are connected by walkways, then they are called "chuanlou" (stringed storied building). In a sequence of halls, the main hall is in the front and the internal hall (nüting, meaning "hall for women") is at back, which mostly has three bays, and is also called "shangfang," meaning the place for owners to reside. In *Gongduan Yingzao Lu*, "shangfang" is called "Two Rooms One Hall" (two bedrooms and a living room). A wing suite or a secret room is usually attached to the three-bay suite, just as the one in Liu's residence at Renfeng Li. Beside the hall, there is a side door with a triangular top, an octagonal gate or a moon gate connected to the parlor or study. The kitchen, storage room and "xiafang" (servants quarters) are located outside the wall for separation from the owners. This layout clearly demonstrates the hierarchy in feudal society. The number of suites and secret rooms depend on the complicatedness of the building. The more complicated the residence, the more suites and secret rooms there will be. *Gongduan Yingzao Lu* observes, "...most halls have three bays. The five-bay halls include the eastern and western rooms on both sides. These wing rooms are called 'suites,' which are usually a secret room, double room, attached room, or boudoir." A small yard is usually located in front of the suite. Parterres are located in the yard. In the summer, the garden is cool with breezes blowing gently; in winter, the yard is warm and the freezing north wind is blocked. This kind of yard layout is very suitable in enclosed residences in Yangzhou. The studies usually have one or two bays, and the larger three-bay building is also used as the parlor. Rockeries and ponds are placed in front of the study, with flowers, trees and bamboos as decoration. Or, a parterre or nursery is placed to create a serene atmosphere. For residences with south-facing main buildings and an eastern or

厅），即所谓"上房"（主人所住的地方），多作三间。《工段营造录》称之为"两房一堂"（两间房，一间起居室），旁边大都置套房，还有再加密室的，如仁丰里刘宅还能见到。厅旁建圭形门、长八方形门或月门，通花厅或书房。墙外附厨房、杂屋及"下房"（仆从居住），使与主人的生活部分隔离，充分反映了封建社会的阶级等级。套房与密室数目的多少据建屋需要的曲折程度而定，越曲折则套房密室越多。《工段营造录》："……三间居多，五间则藏东西梢间于房中，谓之套房，即古密室、复室、连房、闺房之属。"在这类套房前面，皆设小院，置花坛，夏日清风徐来，凉爽宜人，入冬则朔风不到，温暖适居——在封闭性的扬州住宅中，采用这种办法还是切合实际的。书房小者一间、两间，大者兼作花厅，一般都是三间，其前必叠石凿池，点缀花木修竹，或置花坛、药栏等，形成一种极清静的环境。在东门南向或西门南向的住宅中，门屋旁的房屋属账房、书塾及杂屋等次要房屋，这些屋前的天井狭长，仅避日照兼起通风的作用。大门北向的住宅，则以"火巷"为通道，导至前部，进入南向的主屋。

扬州住宅的外观。中型以上的住宅按居住者的地位设照壁，大者用八字照壁，次者一字照壁，最次者在对户他宅的墙上，用壁面隐出方形照壁的形状。华丽的照壁贴水磨面砖，雕刻花纹，正中嵌"福"字，如个园的大门上者，制作精美。外墙以清水砖砌成，讲究的用磨砖对缝做法。门楼用砖砌，加砖刻，最华丽的作八字形，复加斗拱藻井，如东圈门壶园大门即是。一般亦有用平整的磨砖贴面，简洁明快。扬州以"八刻"⁹著世，砖刻即为其中之一。大门髹黑漆，刊红门对，下有门枕石。石刻丰富多彩，大小按居住者的地位而定。屋顶皆作两坡顶，屋脊较高，用漏空脊（屋脊以瓦叠成空花形）。为与高低叠落的山墙相映衬，有时在外墙顶开一排瓦

western gate, secondary buildings are placed by the gate. These buildings are usually for book-keeping, private schooling or storage, in front of which are long and narrow courtyards to block sunlight and improve ventilation. Residences with north-facing gates have fire lanes as corridors to connect the gate with the south-facing main building in the front of the residence.

In order to show the owners' rank, screen walls are placed in front of the gate of medium or large sized residences in Yangzhou. High ranking screen walls are splayed planes in the shape of the Chinese character " 八 ". Low ranking screen walls are in the shape of the Chinese character " 一 ". Even lower ranking screen walls are put on the wall of the opposite house owned by a neighbor. Splendid screen walls' surfaces are made up of finely ground bricks and engraved with patterns. The Chinese character " 福 " is embedded in the center of the screen, like the one in front of Geyuan Garden. The exterior wall is built of shale bricks. More elaborate exterior walls have finely ground bricks. Gate towers are made of bricks, with brick carvings as ornamentation. The most luxurious gate towers are in the shape of the Chinese character " 八 ", with corbel brackets and a caisson ceiling, just like the front gate of the Huyuan Garden at Dongquanmen (East Circle Gate). Normal gate tower surfaces are finished with finely ground bricks so they look simple and bright. Yangzhou is famous for eight types of engraving crafts[9]. Brick carving is one of them. Front gates are painted with a black color. A red inscribed couplet is set on it, with bearing stones at the bottom, and sizes of the couplets depend on the rank of the owner. Rooftops slope on both sides, with a high roof ridge built of latticed tiles. The ridges are contrasted with high and low gable walls. Sometimes, a row of latticed windows is placed at the top of the exterior wall, so that from time to time, tree tops, rattans and vines in the courtyard can be seen from outside. These strategies create organized and refreshing exteriors for the residences, thus adding joy to the lanes.

Passing through the front entrance, there is a village god's shrine with brick engravings. The shrine is built by the wall and looks like real architecture. The engravings are in accordance with the style of the front gate and become the most impressive feature of the inner screen wall. The ground inside the courtyard's pavement is bricks or stones. The second gate is similar to the first. The main hall is tall and lofty and is usually made of high quality fir wood with its original finish. Some large residences' halls use material such as *Phoebe nanmu*, cypress, or *Cyathea spinulosa* as described in the *Gongduan Yingzao Lu*. The timber is usually polished to look smoother and rounder. This kind of unadorned large timber frame structure is in unity with the style of the walls built of shale bricks. The hall portal is decorated with veranda ceilings. The central bay has latticed door leaves and the side bays use removable windows; later, some of the window were replaced by balustrade windows. Internal halls and parlors have only one pair of latticed door leaves in the center, with removable windows on both sides. In the storied halls, walls under the balustrade windows are replaced with railings so that wooden plates could be removed

花窗，可隐约透出院中树梢与藤萝。这些自然形成一种整齐而又清新的外貌，给巷景增加了生趣。

入大门迎面为砖刻土地堂，倚壁而建，外形与真实建筑相似。它的雕刻和大门门楼的形式相协调，是内照壁中最令人注目的。门屋院内以砖或石墁地。二门与大门的形制相类似。厅堂高敞轩豁，一般用质量很高的本色杉木，而大住宅的厅堂又有用楠木、柏木，《工段营造录》载有用桫椤的。木材加工有外施水磨的，更是柔和圆润了。这种存素去华的大木构架与清水砖墙的格调一致。厅堂外檐施翻轩，明间用槅扇，次间和厢房用和合窗。后期的建筑则有改用槛窗的，在内厅与花厅，明间的槅扇只居中用两扇，两旁仍旧用和合窗。楼厅的槛窗，其槛墙改用栏杆，则内装活动的木榻板，在炎热季节可以卸除，以便通风。在分隔上，内院往往以花墙来区分，用地穴（门洞）贯通，地穴有门可开启。

院落的大小与建筑物高度的比例一般为 1:1，这个比例在扬州地区能保证有充分的日照。夏日上加凉棚，前后门牖洞开，清风自引，从地穴中来的兜风更是凉爽。到冬季将地穴门关闭，阳光满阶，便不觉有严寒的侵袭了。这些花墙与重重的门户增加了庭院空间感与深度，有小宅不见其狭、大宅不觉其旷的好处，在解决功能的前提下，同时又扩大了艺术效果。大厅的院子用横长形，有的配上两厢或两廊，使主体突出。内厅都带两厢，院子形成方形。房屋进深一般比苏南浅，北面甚至有不设窗牖的，因夏季较凉爽，冬季在室内需要较多日照的缘故。

对于室内的空间处理，主要是希望达到有分有合，曲折有度，使用灵活，人处其间觉含蓄不尽的设计意图。因此在花厅中，必用罩或槅扇，划成似分非分、可大可小的空间，既有主次，又有变化。如仁丰里辛园、地官第汪氏小苑中皆可见到。厅室前面的

during hot months to improve ventilation. Latticed walls are usually used to separate inner courtyards, which are connected by door openings.

In Yangzhou, the ratio between the size of the courtyard and the height of the building is usually 1:1 to ensure there is substantial daylight. In summertime, a sun shed is set up in the courtyard, with the front and back gates and windows open to let in the cool breeze. The air coming from the door opening in the wall feels particularly cool. In wintertime, the door opening in the wall is closed so that sunlight is enclosed in the courtyard, warming up the harsh winter. These latticed walls and layers of doors adds spaciousness and depth to the courtyards so that small residences don't seem so narrow and large residences not so empty. This spatial strategy not only meets functional needs, but also enhances artistic effects. The central hall's courtyard is in the shape of a long rectangle, some of which include two wings or corridors to highlight the central part. The internal halls all have wing rooms and the courtyards are square-shaped. Their depths are usually shallower than the internal halls in South Jiangsu and some of the rooms don't even have windows on the north side. Thus, the rooms feel cool and refreshing in summer, and daylight is extended in winter.

The interior layout should be both open and close, twisted and straight, and with flexibility so that people inside feel there is always more room. Therefore, the parlor is segmented with hanging latticed screens or latticed door leaves so spaces are in-between the sense of attached and detached, small and large. In this way, the major space is highlighted and full of variations. Examples can be found in Xinyuan Garden at Renfeng Li and Wangshi Xiaoyuan at Diguandi. The building with a larger depth might have a veranda ceiling with two archs, like the example in Lu's residence on Kangshan Street. An inner room is the major room, which is both connected and disconnected with the attached side rooms. The inner room is also separated from wing rooms with hanging latticed screens or latticed door leaves. The hanging screens are usually round and hollow, and some of them are covered with exquisitely crafted patterned mesh. Studies can be freely segmented. Halls don't have ceilings, nor rough frames (double roofs). Some residential rooms have fixed ceilings. Some parlors have arched ceilings. All the rooms are paved with square bricks, whose four corners are elevated and the hollow between the bricks and the ground is filled in with yellow sand (as in vol.1 of *Changwu Zhi*). Finely ground bricks are laid on the edges so that the floor can be kept flat and prevent the risk of mold. In winter, bedrooms are covered with a mobile wooden floor to keep the room warm, which also reduces the clear height of the room. Some high-quality storied halls have brick floor in rooms on upper floor, with a removable wooden floor to silence the footstep. Walking in these rooms embodies the strategy from *Changwu Zhi* in that "it feels just like walking on the floor of a single-story house."

Interior walls and exterior walls are both made of brick. High quality houses use ganged bricks. Residences with smaller budgets striving for a clear appearance use bricks of various sizes with mortar. Exterior walls, if as tall as man's average height, are filleted round for traffic

翻轩，在进深较大的建筑中有用二卷（两个翻轩）的，如康山街卢宅。内室与套房有主副之别，似合又分，又内室往往连厢房，而以罩或槅扇分间。罩以圆光罩（罩作圆形的）为多，有的还施纱槅（罩的花纹中夹纱），雕刻多数精美。书房中亦可自由划分，应用上均较灵活。厅堂皆露明造（不用天花），亦不施草架（用两层屋顶）；居住房屋有酌用天花的；花厅内部亦有作轩顶（卷棚）。房屋内均墁方砖，用砖下四角置覆钵的"空铺"法（见《长物志》卷一），垫黄沙，磨砖对缝，既平且无潮湿之患。卧室内，冬天上置木地屏（方形木制装脚的活动地板）保暖，同时亦减低了室内空间的净高。有些质量高的楼厅，二层亦墁砖，更有再加上地屏的，能使履步无声，与明代《长物志》卷一上所说办法"与平屋无异"相符合。

内外墙都用砖实砌，在质量高的住宅中用清水砖，经济性的住宅则用灰泥拼砌大小不等的杂砖，外表也很整齐。为了便利交通，外墙的转角在一人高的地方使用抹角砌。廊壁部分刷白，内壁用木护壁，其余仍保存砖的本色。天井铺地通常用砖石。砖铺有方砖、条砖平铺及条砖仄铺。石铺则用石板与冰裂纹铺，更有用大方块大理石、高资石拼铺的。柱础用"古镜"式，在明代及清代早期的建筑中还沿用了"磉"形石础，大住宅皆用"石鼓"，或再置垫"覆盆"础石，取材用高资石兼有大理石的。

柱均为直柱。明代住宅的柱顶尚存"卷杀"（曲线）的手法，比例肥硕。柱径与柱高的比例约为1:9，如大东门毛宅大厅，现在一般见到的比例在1:10～1:16之间。柱的排列与《工段营造录》所说"厅堂无中柱，住屋有中柱"一致。大厅明间有用通长额枋，而减去平柱两根的，此为便利观剧，不阻碍视线。梁架做法可分为三种：一是苏南的扁作做法；二是圆料直材，在扬州最为普遍；三是介于直梁与月梁（略呈弯形的梁）间的介体，将直

convenience. Corridors' walls are partially painted white, and internal walls are covered with wooden wainscot, with bricks preserved with their original colors. Courtyard grounds are mainly covered with square or rectangular bricks, or stone plates in cracked-ice patterns, large square marble slabs or stone plates from Gaozi. Column bases are shaped as an "ancient mirror." In the Ming and the early Qing Dynasties, block stones were also used in buildings. Large residences all use "stone drums," some of which are placed on top of stone bases like "overturned basin" made of stones from Gaozi or marble.

All the columns are straight columns. Capitals of columns in residences from Ming were designed in the style of "round off," which makes the column look thick and robust. The column's ratio between diameter and height is about 1:9, just as the ones in the grand hall of Mao's residence at Dadongmen. Nowadays, the ratio usually lies in between 1:10 to 1:16. Columns are laid out following the description from *Gongduan Yingzao Lu* with "no columns in halls, but in residing rooms." The central bay of a hall has a full-length horizontal tablet minus two central columns to facilitate the view of the audience watching performances in the room. There are generally three styles of building beam frames. First, timber with rectangle cross section, which is seen in South Jiangsu area. Second, round timber, which is the most common in Yangzhou. The third one is the kind in-between a straight beam and a moon beam (a beam that is slightly curved). The lower part of both ends of the straight beam is rounded. This style seems to be influenced by Anhui architecture. The second style is the most representative of

Yangzhou buildings. Apart from the three styles, Wu's residence at Beihexia is designed by a Ningbo craftsman, which might be the only case in its unique style. Round timber was used as the beam and joints are crafted with precision. For regular halls, the beam frame is made up of a five-purlin beam between the front and back columns. Short columns sit on top of the beam, and then a three-purlin beam and a small pillar sit on top of the short columns. However, square beams and subplate are not placed under the purlins, which is not the same as the example in *Gongduan Yingzao Lu*; therefore, it is probably a method from North Jiangsu area. From a structural perspective, this method is not thoughtful enough. Some parlors have six pairs of round ridges with gable walls of changing heights rounded in the upper part. Some luxurious halls use square columns and beams, following the style of the "square hall" mentioned in *Gongduan Yingzao Lu*. Veranda ceilings are in various shapes; normally the rafters are curved into the shape of "crabapple tree flower" or "water chestnut," and also "crane's neck" or "boat's awning." Rough frames are used infrequently.

Balustrades are usually tall in Yangzhou residences. Patterns of the lattices for the balustrades are mostly in the shape of a reel, surrounded with convex moldings on four sides. The hanging fascia under the eaves are mostly simple. Both are in accordance with the exterior façades of the buildings. Rooftop tiles are paved on top of sheathing tiles, and the tile ends are thick and robust for decoration and drainage purpose. The ends of arched tiles have longer lower parts and the plate tiles are elevated in the upper parts.

梁的两端略做"卷杀"，下刻弧线，此种做法看来似受徽式建筑的影响。以上三种做法中以第二种最代表扬州的风格。尚有北河下吴宅，建筑系出宁波匠师之手，应当是孤例了。圆料的梁架用材挺健，而接头处的卯榫砍杀尤精，很是准确。一般厅堂，主要梁架在前后柱间施五架梁，上置蜀柱，再安三架梁与脊瓜柱，不过檩下不施枋及垫板，与《工段营造录》所示不符，当为苏北地方做法，从结构上来说，似有不够周到的地方。花厅有用六架卷棚的，其山墙作圆形叠落式。豪华的厅堂有改为方柱方梁的，系《工段营造录》所谓"方厅之制"。翻轩一般为海棠轩（椽子弯作海棠形）与菱角轩（椽子弯作菱角状），但多变例。此外，鹤颈轩（椽子弯如鹤颈）也有见到，但以船篷轩为多。草架只偶用在翻轩之上。

栏杆的比例一般较高，花纹常用拐子纹，四周起凸形线脚。檐下挂落也很简洁。两者都与整个建筑立面保持协调。屋顶在望砖上甋瓦，其瓦饰有勾头、滴水等。勾头的下部较长，滴水的上部加高，形式渐趋厚重。

扬州城区住宅的给水问题，除小秦淮与汶河一带有河水可使用外，住宅内皆有水井，少者一口，多者几口，其位置有在院子中、厨房前、园中或"火巷"内，更有掘在屋内的暗井（无井栏）。坊巷中的公共用井随处可见。凡在井的边墙，必砌发券（杭绍一带用竖立石板），以免墙身下陷，也是他处所罕见的。井水除洗涤及供饮用外，必要时还可作消防用水。此外，住宅内还置有存储檐漏以供食用的"天落水缸"，它与供消防用的储水缸并备。每宅院子中有阴井，在大门外有总的下水道。

扬州的住宅多与园林、庭院相结合，两者有分有合，不可孤立言之。住宅中的庭院绿化可参看园林部分，兹不赘述了。

Regarding water supply for residences in the city of Yangzhou, Xiaoqinhuai River and Wen River's water could both be utilized. Every residence also has a water well, some even have multiple wells. The location of the water well could be in the courtyard, in front of the kitchen, in the garden or inside the fire lane. There also exist hidden wells inside rooms (without well stop). Public wells in the lanes could be found everywhere. Brick arches are built into the lower sections of the walls beside the wells (vertical stone plates are used in Hangzhou and Shaoxing) to prevent the walls from sinking, and the brick arches are rarely seen elsewhere. Water from the well is used for cleaning and drinking, and also for fire emergencies when needed. Inside the residences, rainwater is also preserved in water vats under the eaves for store drinking water. There are also water vats for putting out fires. Hidden wells are built into the courtyards to be connected to the main sewage outside the front doors.

Yangzhou's residences are complemented well with gardens and courtyards. Buildings and gardens are sometimes combined and sometimes detached; none should be left alone. For the greening in the residences, the reader can refer to paragraphs about the garden, so I won't go into details.

Residences in Yangzhou look tidy and clean from the exterior, which greatly impacts the overall appearance for the city. There are not that many organized residential blocks in Chinese ancient cities. Yangzhou residences are bright and serene, with smaller ones nested in larger ones with great flexibility. Spatially, courtyards are segmented—wide and narrow spaces are grouped skillfully. Daylight and ventilation are handled with care. Buildings, regardless of the scale, have appropriate functions and orderly proportions. Site areas are economically allocated so that residents feel comfortable and visitors feel pleasant. Building plans are adapted to the sites with careful programming. No matter what kind of orientation the sites have, the houses can always face south. Whether the sites are large or small, the spaces can always be combined appropriately to satisfy functional needs. The architectural style is a combination of the south and the north, with a particular focus on order. These sum up the characteristics of residences in Yangzhou.

Yangzhou's gardens and residences are of great value to Chinese architecture history, and also serve as important materials for research on Yangzhou's economy and cultural development, especially the working class's achievements in architecture and landscape architecture. These materials can be references for research on contemporary landscape architecture.

扬州住宅建筑在外观上修整挺健，对维护良好的城市面貌起到一定作用，这许多井然有序的居住区在我国旧城市中还是较少有的。它的优点是明洁宁静，大中寓小，分合自如。在空间处理上，注意到院落分隔与宽狭的组合，以及日照与通风的合理解决。建筑物不论大小，都配置恰当，比例匀整，用地面积亦称经济，达到居之者适、观之者畅的目的。在平面处理上，能因地制宜，巧于安排，不论何种朝向的地形，皆能得到南向；不论何种大小的地形，皆能有较好的空间组合，并解决功能上的需要。当地的建筑手法介于南北两地之间，以工整见长。以上都是扬州住宅的特征。

扬州的园林与住宅在我国建筑史上有着重要的价值，也是研究扬州经济与文化发展的重要资料，尤其是古代劳动人民在园林建筑方面的成就，可供现代园林建筑研究与借鉴。

平山堂
大明寺

小金山

瘦

西

湖

大虹桥

梅岭西园

天宁寺

史公祠

荷花池

扬州市区示意图

| Sketch map of Yangzhou

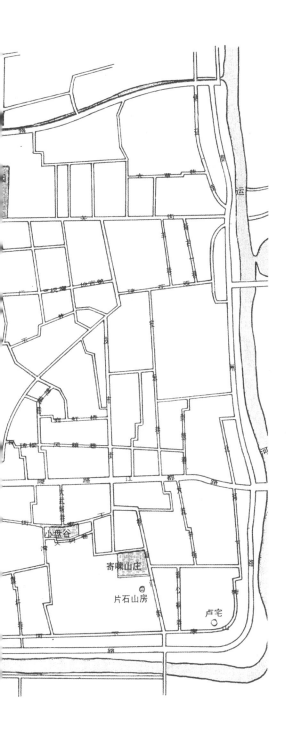

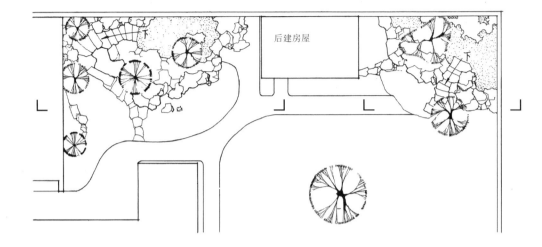

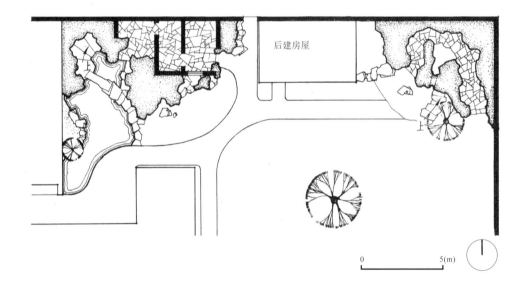

后建房屋

后建房屋

0       5(m)

0    2(m)

对页上：片石山房屋顶平面图
对页中：片石山房底层平面图
对页下：西部假山立面图

Opposite top: Roof plan of Pianshi Shanfang
Opposite middle: Ground floor plan of Pianshi Shanfang
Opposite bottom: Elevation of the artificial moutains in the west section

1. 竹西佳处门 | Zhuxi Jiachu Gate
2. 润碧门 | Runbi Gate
3. 丛书楼 | Congshu Tower
4. 透风漏月厅 | Toufeng-louyue Hall
5. 个园门 | Geyuan Gate
6. 觅句廊 | Miju Corridor
7. 宜雨轩（桂花厅）| Yiyu Veranda
(Osmanthus Hall)
8. 清漪亭 | Qingyi Pavilion
9. 抱山楼（"壶天自春"，即七间楼）|
Baoshan Tower ("Hutianzichun", the seven-
bay storied building)
10. 鹤亭 | Crane Pavilion
11. 裱画社 | Painting mounting house
12. 花房 | Greenhouse
13. 复道廊 | Two-storied walkway
14. 拂云亭 | Fuyun Pavilion
15. 住秋阁 | Zhuqiu Belvedere
16. 读书处 | Dushuchu

0    5(m)

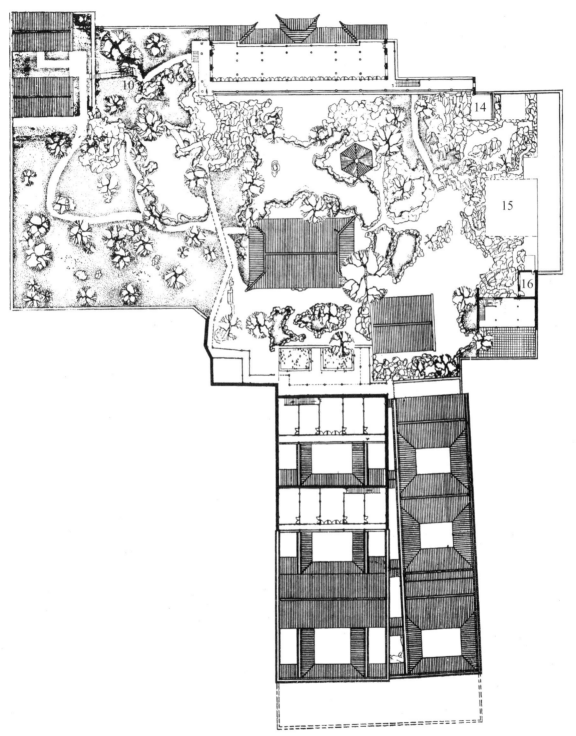

对页：个园底层平面图
本页：个园二层平面图

Opposite: Ground floor plan of Geyuan Garden
This page: First floor plan of Geyuan Garden

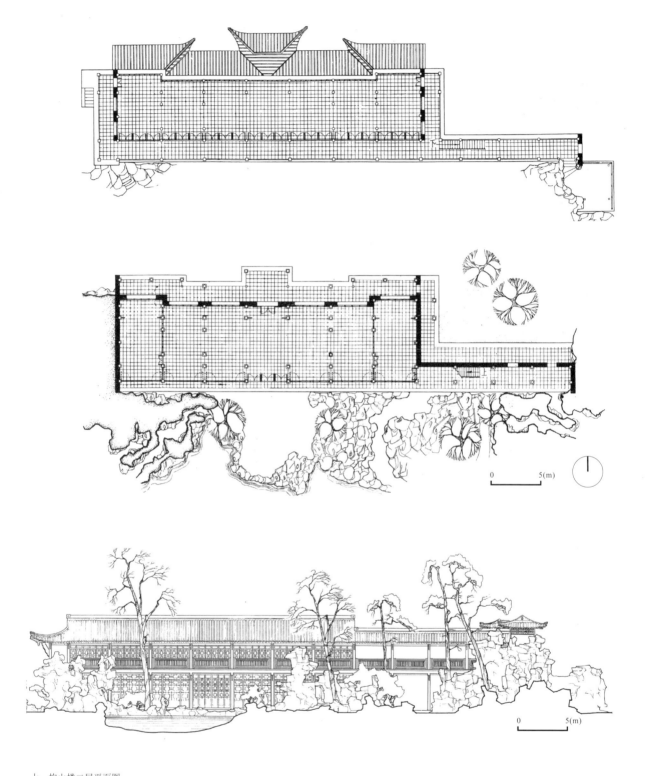

上：抱山楼二层平面图
中：抱山楼底层平面图
下：抱山楼南立面图

Top: First floor plan of Baoshan Tower
Middle: Ground floor plan of Baoshan Tower
Bottom: South elevation of Baoshan Tower

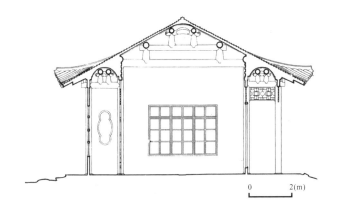

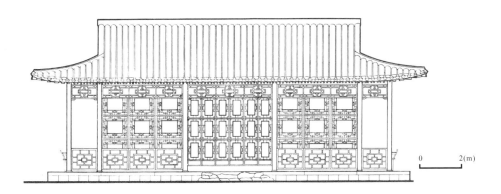

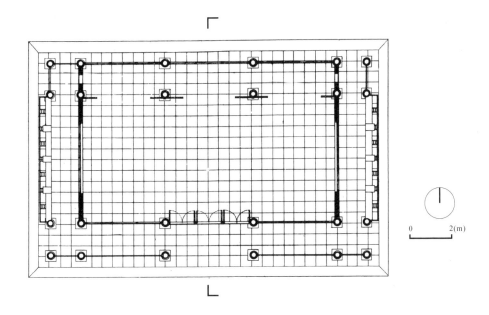

上：宜雨轩剖面图
中：宜雨轩南立面图
下：宜雨轩平面图

Top: Section of Yiyu Veranda
Middle: South elevation of Yiyu Veranda
Bottom: Plan of Yiyu Veranda

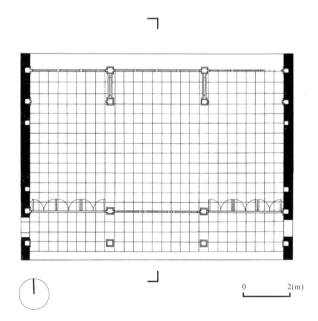

0        2(m)

0        2(m)

上：个园剖面图
下左：个园照壁平面图与剖面图
下右：透风漏月厅平面图

Top: Section of Geyuan Garden
Bottom left: Plan and section of the screen wall in Geyuan Garden
Bottom right: Plan of Toufeng-louyue Hall

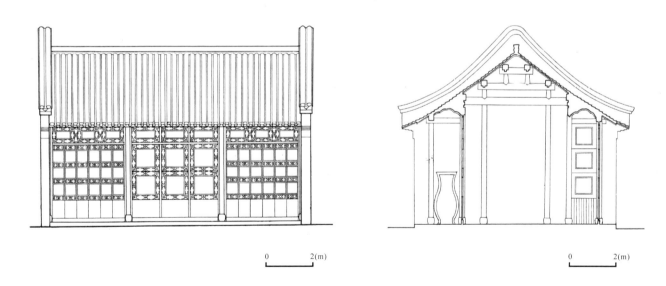

下左：透风漏月厅南立面图
下右：透风漏月厅剖面图

Bottom left: South elevation of Toufeng-louyue Hall
Bottom right: Section of Toufeng-louyue Hall

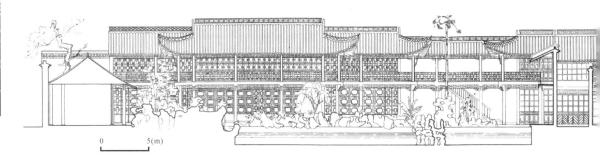

0      5(m)

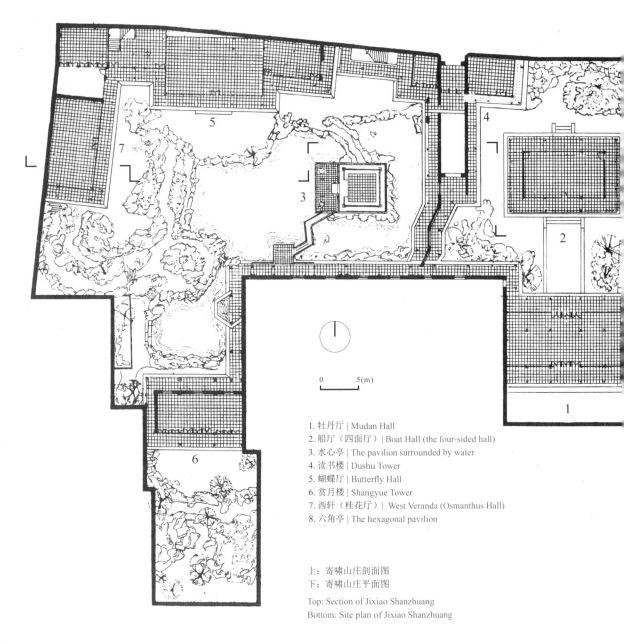

0      5(m)

1. 牡丹厅 | Mudan Hall
2. 船厅（四面厅）| Boat Hall (the four-sided hall)
3. 水心亭 | The pavilion surrounded by water
4. 读书楼 | Dushu Tower
5. 蝴蝶厅 | Butterfly Hall
6. 赏月楼 | Shangyue Tower
7. 西轩（桂花厅）| West Veranda (Osmanthus Hall)
8. 六角亭 | The hexagonal pavilion

上：寄啸山庄剖面图
下：寄啸山庄平面图

Top: Section of Jixiao Shanzhuang
Bottom: Site plan of Jixiao Shanzhuang

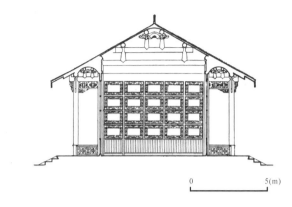

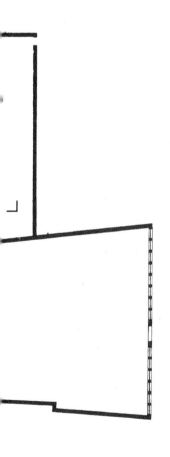

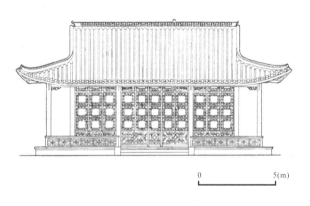

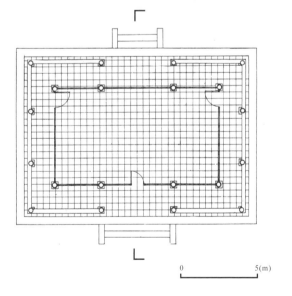

上：四面厅剖面图
中：四面厅南立面图
下：四面厅平面图

Top: Section of the four-sided hall
Middle: South elevation of the four-sided hall
Bottom: Plan of the four-sided hall

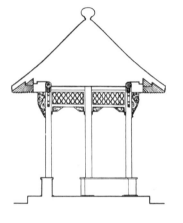
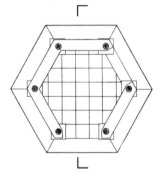

上：六角亭立面图
中：六角亭剖面图
下：六角亭平面图

Top: Elevation of the hexagonal pavilion
Middle: Section of the hexagonal pavilion
Bottom: Plan of the hexagonal pavilion

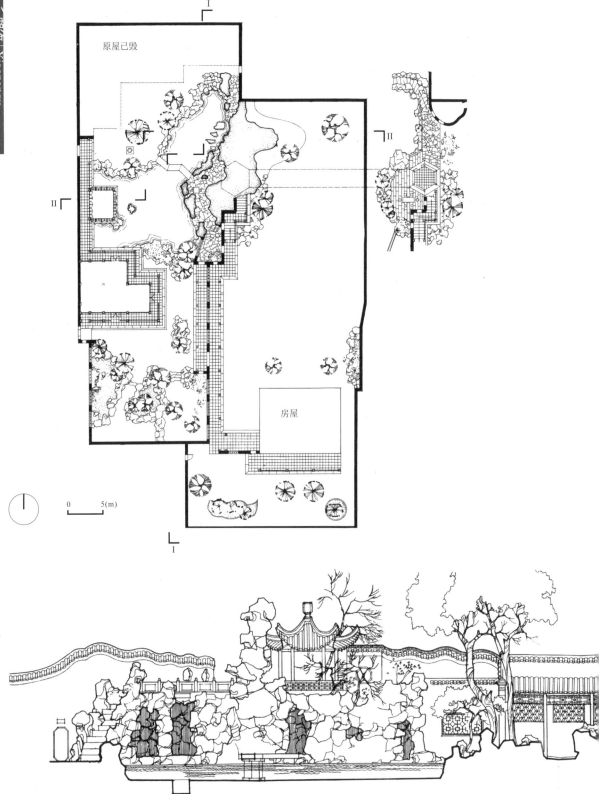

原屋已毁

房屋

0    5(m)

上：小盘谷平面图
下：小盘谷 I—I 剖面图

Top: Site plan of Xiaopangu
Bottom: Section of Xiaopangu I-I

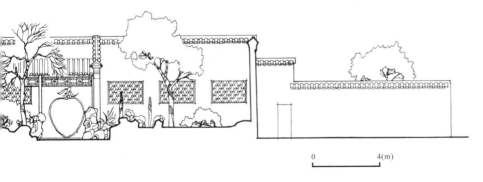

中：小盘谷 II—II 剖面图

Middle: Section of Xiaopangu II-II

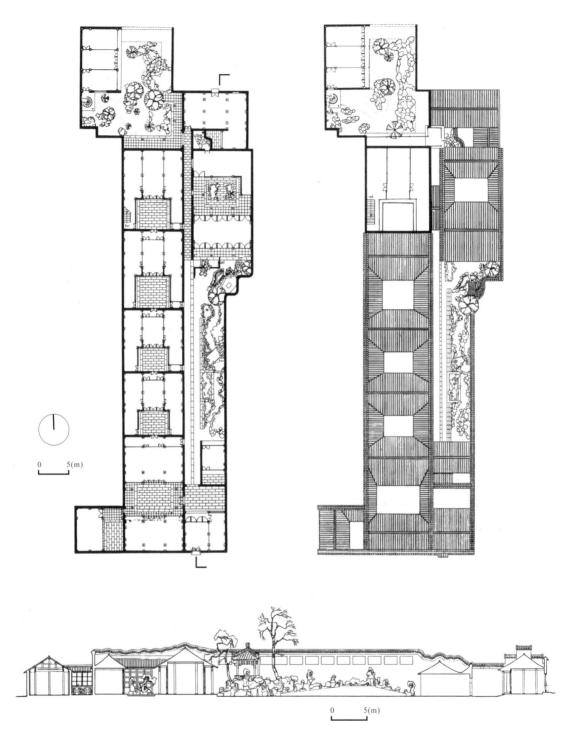

0    5(m)

0    5(m)

上左：逸圃底层平面图
上右：逸圃二层平面图
下：逸圃剖面图

Top left: Ground floor plan of Yipu
Top right: First floor plan of Yipu
Bottom: Section of Yipu

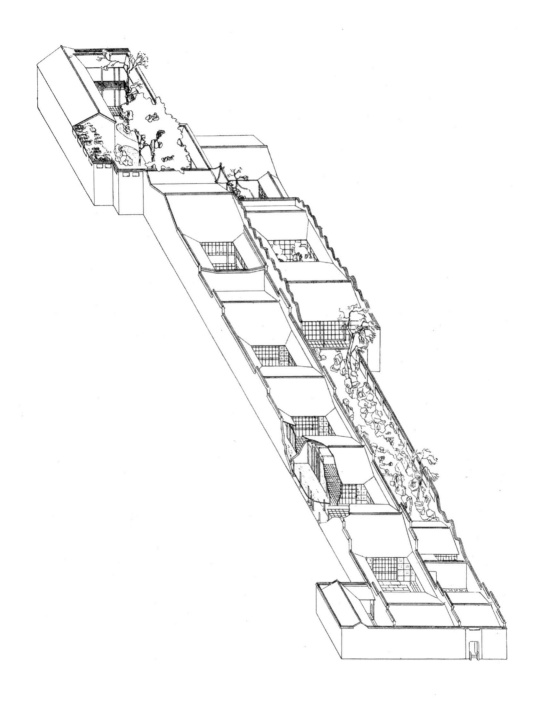

逸圃轴测图

Axonometric drawing of Yipu

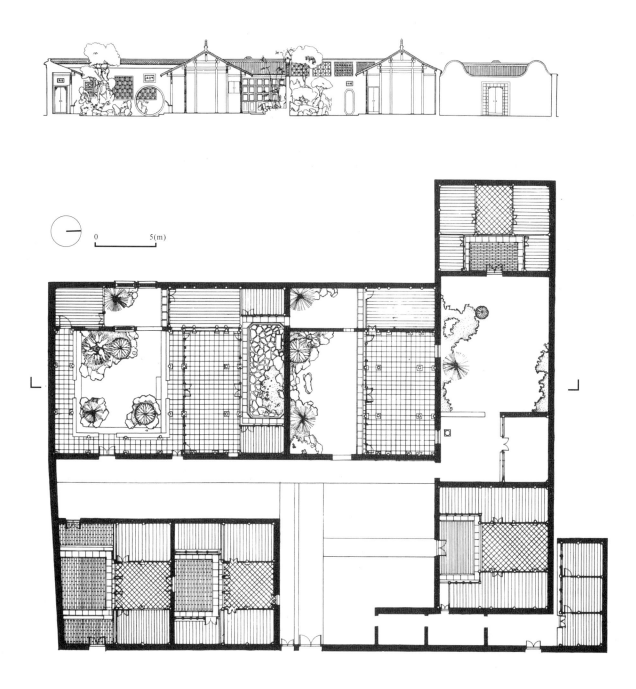

上：怡庐剖面图
下：怡庐平面图

Top: Section of Yilu
Bottom: Site plan of Yilu

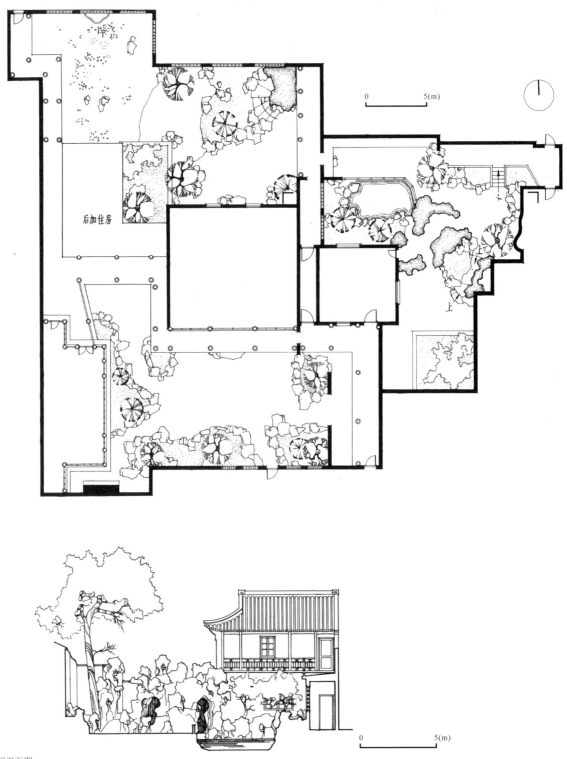

后加住房

0     5(m)

上

0     5(m)

上：余园平面图
下：余园剖面图

Top: Site plan of Yuyuan Garden
Bottom: Section of Yuyuan Garden

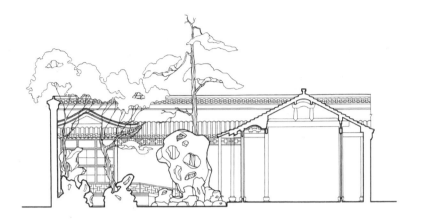

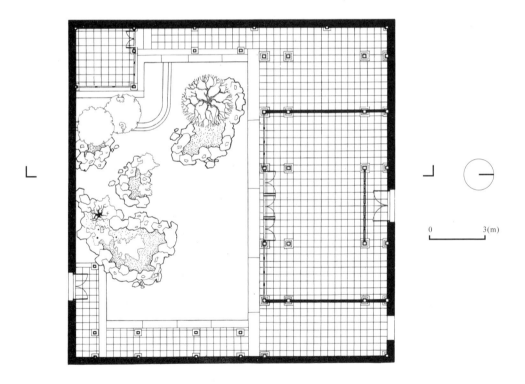

上：蔚圃剖面图
下：蔚圃平面图

Top: Section of Weipu
Bottom: Site plan of Weipu

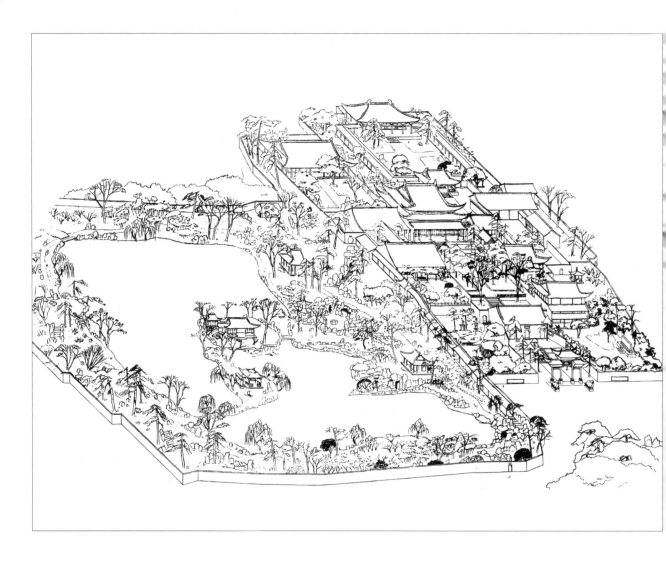

大明寺轴测图

Axonometric drawing of Daming Temple

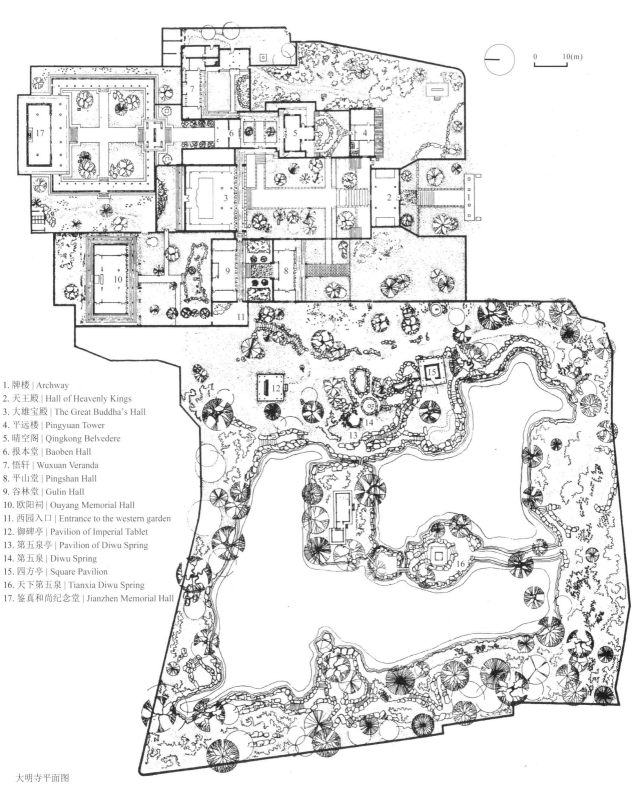

1. 牌楼 | Archway
2. 天王殿 | Hall of Heavenly Kings
3. 大雄宝殿 | The Great Buddha's Hall
4. 平远楼 | Pingyuan Tower
5. 晴空阁 | Qingkong Belvedere
6. 报本堂 | Baoben Hall
7. 悟轩 | Wuxuan Veranda
8. 平山堂 | Pingshan Hall
9. 谷林堂 | Gulin Hall
10. 欧阳祠 | Ouyang Memorial Hall
11. 西园入口 | Entrance to the western garden
12. 御碑亭 | Pavilion of Imperial Tablet
13. 第五泉亭 | Pavilion of Diwu Spring
14. 第五泉 | Diwu Spring
15. 四方亭 | Square Pavilion
16. 天下第五泉 | Tianxia Diwu Spring
17. 鉴真和尚纪念堂 | Jianzhen Memorial Hall

大明寺平面图

Site plan of Daming Temple

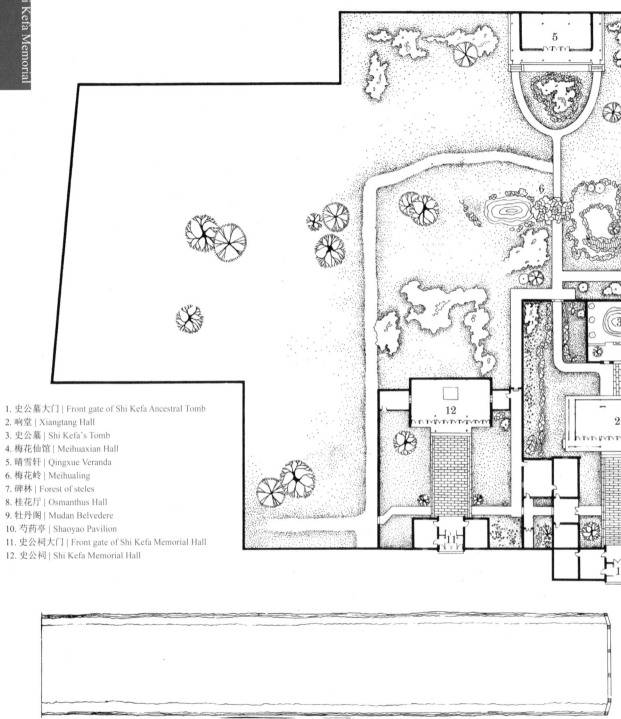

1. 史公墓大门 | Front gate of Shi Kefa Ancestral Tomb
2. 响堂 | Xiangtang Hall
3. 史公墓 | Shi Kefa's Tomb
4. 梅花仙馆 | Meihuaxian Hall
5. 晴雪轩 | Qingxue Veranda
6. 梅花岭 | Meihualing
7. 碑林 | Forest of steles
8. 桂花厅 | Osmanthus Hall
9. 牡丹阁 | Mudan Belvedere
10. 芍药亭 | Shaoyao Pavilion
11. 史公祠大门 | Front gate of Shi Kefa Memorial Hall
12. 史公祠 | Shi Kefa Memorial Hall

史公祠平面图

Site plan of Shi Kefa Memorial

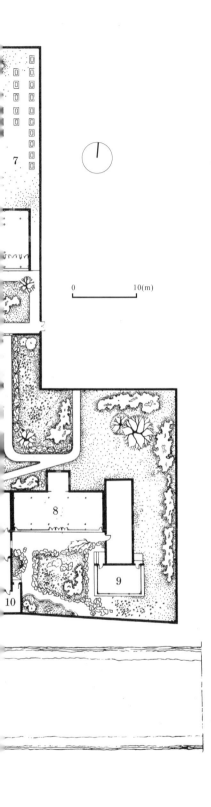

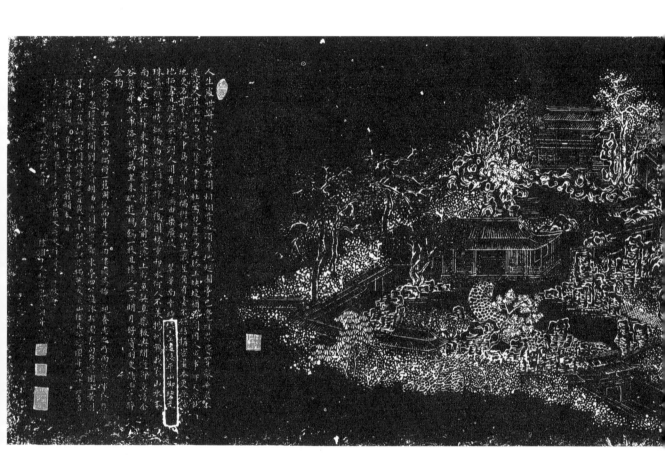

棣园图拓本

Rubbing edition of the *Drawing of Diyuan Garden*

172

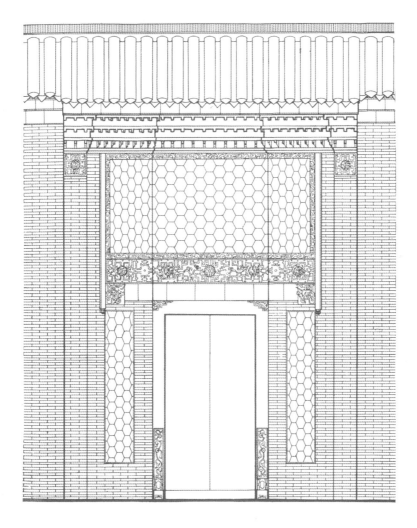

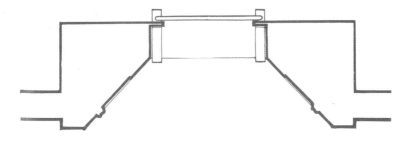

东圈门二十二号大门立面图与平面图

Elevation and plan of the front gate of No. 22 Dongquanmen

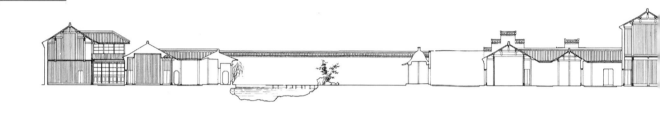

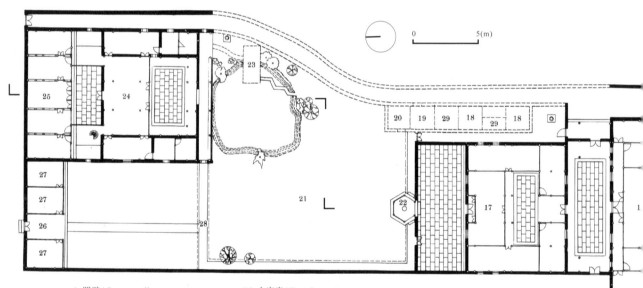

1. 照壁 | Screen wall
2. 大门 | Front gate
3. 门堂 | Gate hall
4. 门房 | Gate house
5. 老师宿舍 | Teachers' dormitory
6. 火巷 | Fire lane
7. 对厅 | Converse hall
8. 客房 | Guest room
9. 书房 | Study
10. 大厅 | Main hall
11. 花厅 | Parlor
12. 二厅 | Second hall
13. 账房 | Accounting room
14. 女厅 | Nüting
15. 内账房 | Inner accounting room

16. 女客房 | Female guest room
17. 内宅 | Inner residence
18. 厨房 | Kitchen
19. 柴房 | Storage
20. 厕所 | Privy
21. 意园 | Yiyuan
22. 亭子 | Pavilion
23. 旱船 | Land boat
24. 后厅 | Rear hall
25. 藏书楼 | Library
26. 后门堂 | Rear gate hall
27. 后门房 | Rear gate house
28. 廊子 | Corridor
29. 天井 | Small yard

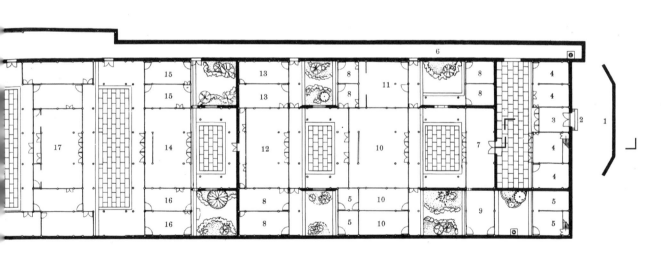

上：康山街卢宅剖面图
下：康山街卢宅底层平面图

Top: Section of Lu's residence on Kangshan Street
Bottom: Ground floor plan of Lu's residence on Kangshan Street

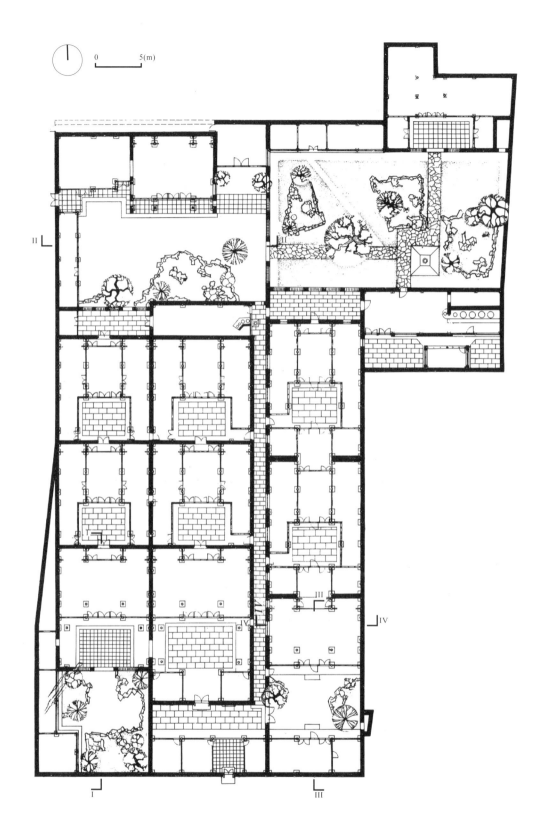

0    5(m)

汪氏小苑平面图

Site plan of Wangshi Xiaoyuan

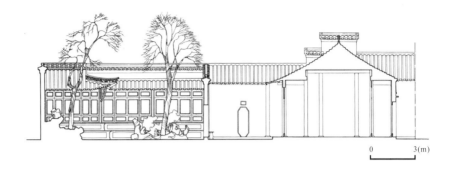

I—I 剖面图
Section I-I

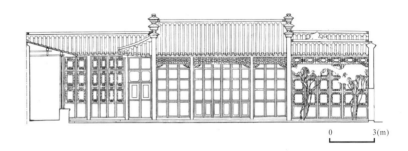

II—II 剖面图
Section II-II

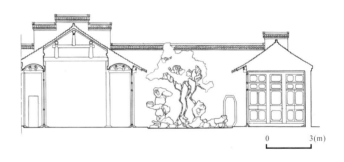

III—III 剖面图
Section III-III

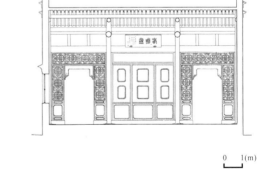

下左：花厅装饰详图
下右：IV-IV 花厅剖面图

Bottom left: Detail drawing of decaration of the parlor
Bottom right: Section of the parlor IV-IV

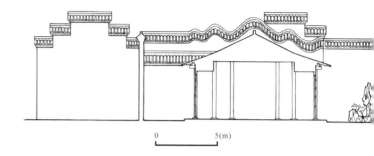

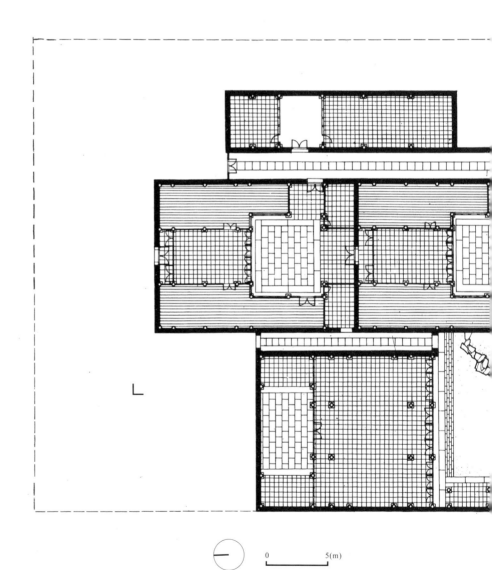

上：赞化宫赵宅剖面图
下：赞化宫赵宅平面图

Top: Section of Zhao's residence at Zanhuagong
Bottom: Site plan of Zhao's residence at Zanhuagong

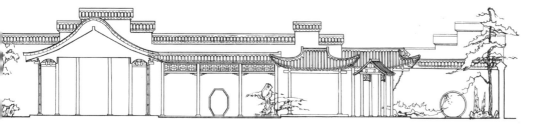

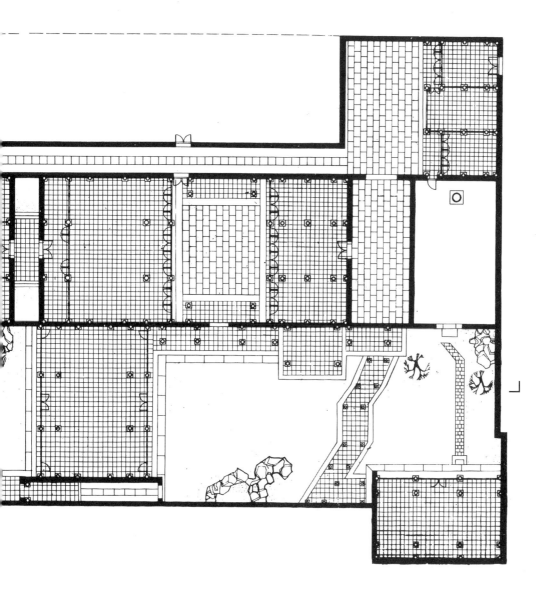

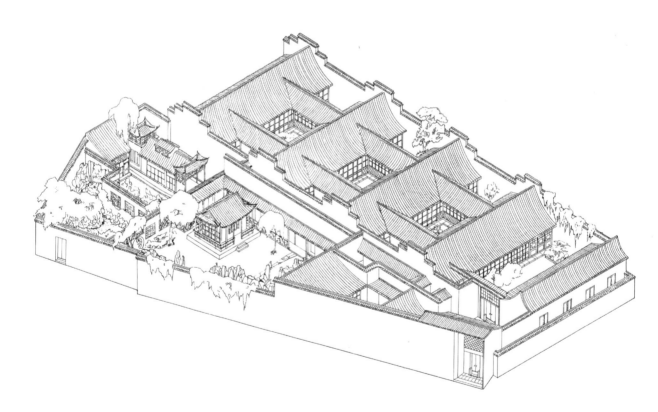

永胜街魏宅轴测图

Axonometric drawing of Wei's residence on Yongsheng Street

0    4(m)

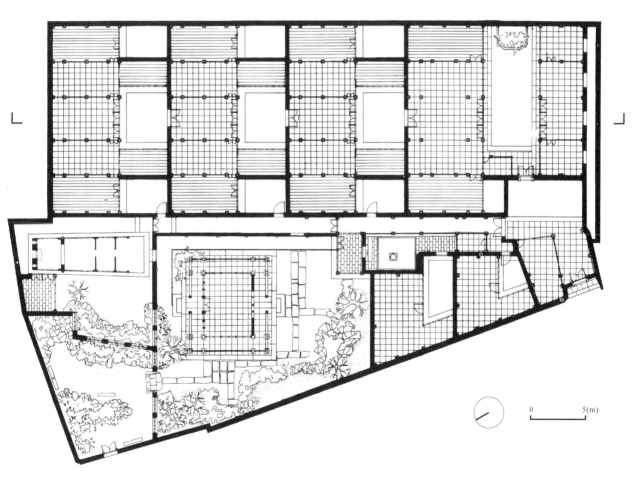

0    5(m)

上：永胜街魏宅剖面图
下：永胜街魏宅平面图

Top: Section of Wei's residence on Yongsheng Street
Bottom: Site plan of Wei's residence on Yongsheng Street

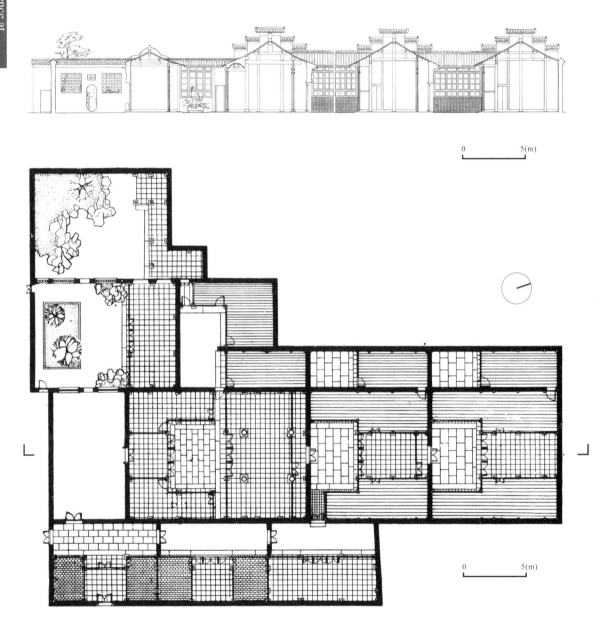

0    5(m)

0    5(m)

上：仁丰里刘宅剖面图
下：仁丰里刘宅平面图

Top: Section of Liu's residence at Renfeng Li
Bottom: Site plan of Liu's residence at Renfeng Li

对页上左：大武城巷贾宅二层平面图
对页上右：大武城巷贾宅底层平面图
对页下：大武城巷贾宅剖面图

Opposite top left: First floor plan of Jia's residence at Dawucheng Xiang
Opposite top right: Ground floor plan of Jia's residence at Dawucheng Xiang
Opposite bottom: Section of Jia's residence at Dawucheng Xiang

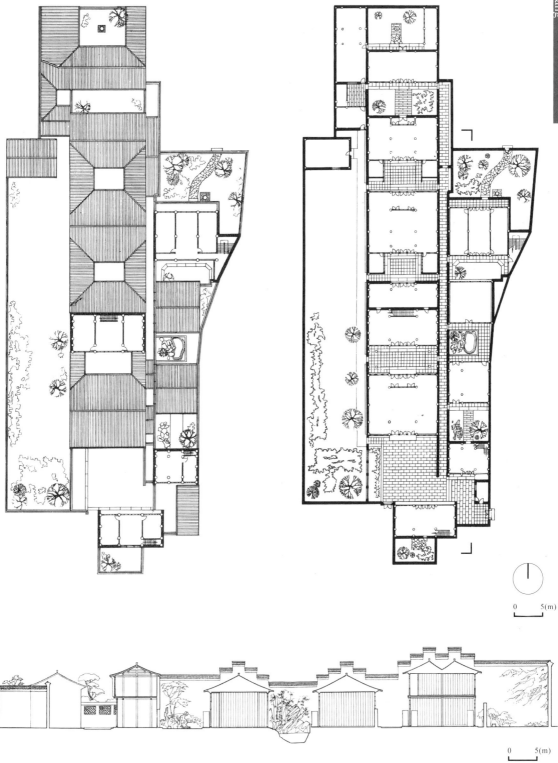

0    5(m)

0    5(m)

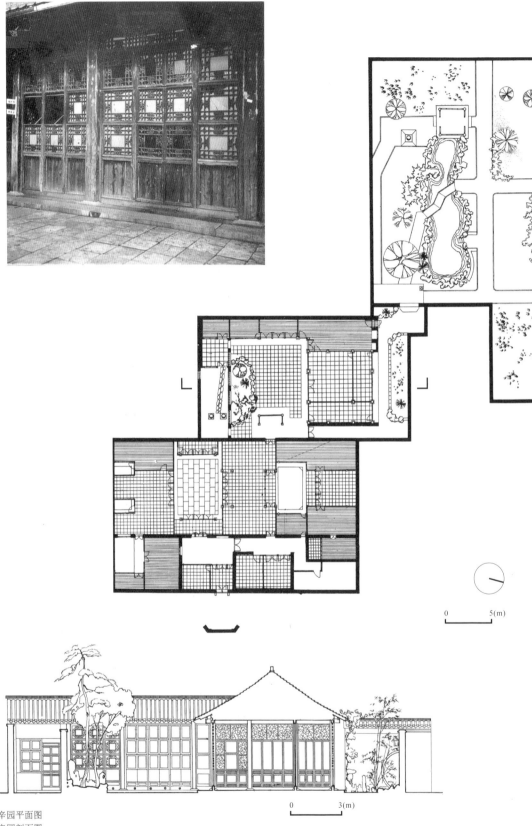

中：仁丰里辛园平面图
下：仁丰里辛园剖面图

Middle: Site plan of Xinyuan Garden at Renfeng Li
Bottom: Section of Xinyuan Garden at Renfeng Li

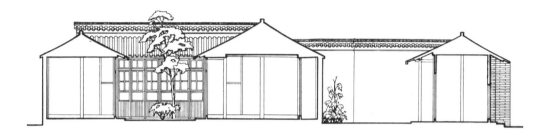

上：石牌楼黄氏汉庐剖面图
下：石牌楼黄氏汉庐平面图

Top: Section of Huangshi Hanlu at Shipailou
Bottom: Site plan of Huangshi Hanlu at Shipailou

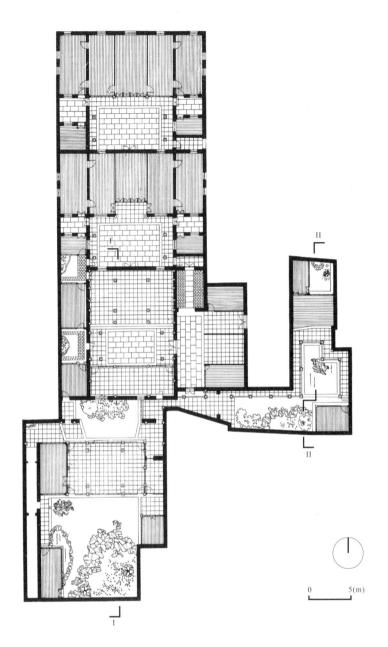

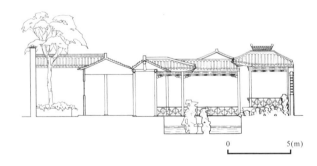

上：甘泉路匏庐平面图
下：甘泉路匏庐 II—II 剖面图
对页下：甘泉路匏庐 I—I 剖面图

Top: Site plan of Paolu on Ganquan Road
Bottom: Section of Paolu on Ganquan Road II-II
Opposite bottom: Section of Paolu on Ganquan Road I-I

0    5(m)

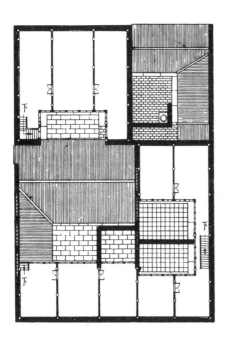

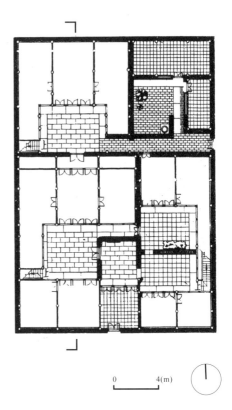

0    4(m)

上：丁家湾某宅剖面图
下左：丁家湾某宅二层平面图
下右：丁家湾某宅底层平面图

Top: Section of the residential compound at Dingjiawan
Bottom left: First floor plan of the residential compound at Dingjiawan
Bottom right: Ground floor plan of the residential compound at Dingjiawan

194

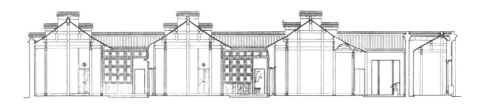

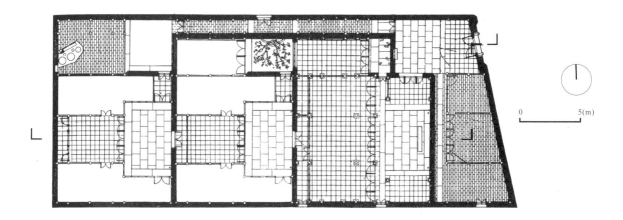

中：丁家湾许宅剖面图
下：丁家湾许宅平面图

Middle: Section of Xu's residence at Dingjiawan
Bottom: Site plan of Xu's residence at Dingjiawan

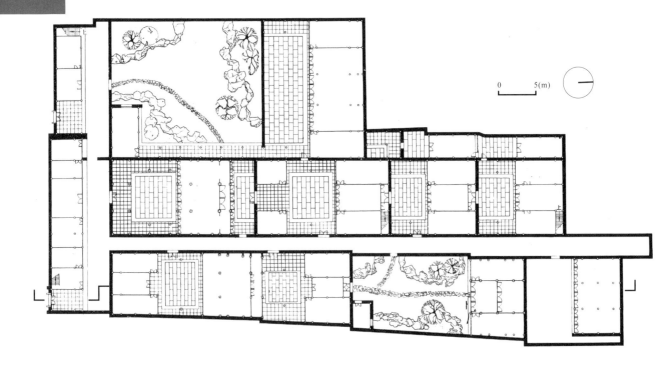

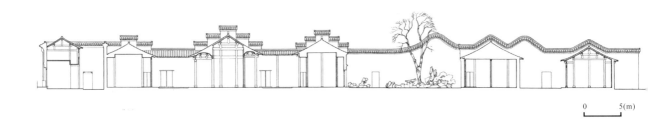

上：地官第十二号某宅平面图
下：地官第十二号某宅剖面图

Top: Site plan of a residence at No. 12 Diguandi
Bottom: Section of a residence at No. 12 Diguandi

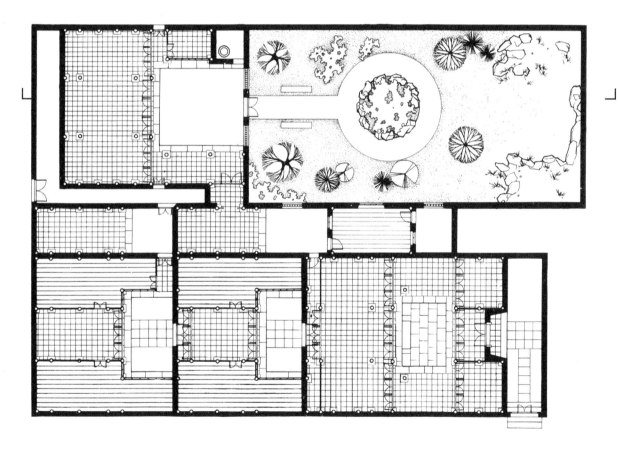

上：弥陀巷赵宅剖面图
下：弥陀巷赵宅平面图

Top: Section of Zhao`s residence at Mituo Xiang
Bottom: Site plan of Zhao`s residence at Mituo Xiang

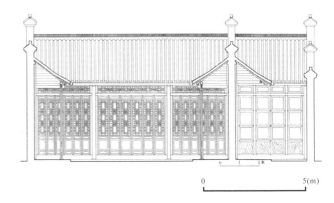

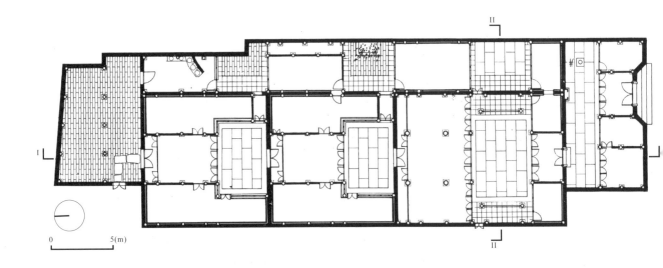

上：小武城巷许宅 II—II 剖面图
中：小武城巷许宅 I—I 剖面图
下：小武城巷许宅平面图

Top: Section of Xu's residence at Xiaowucheng Xiang II-II
Middle: Section of Xu's residence at Xiaowucheng Xiang I-I
Bottom: Site plan of Xu's residence at Xiaowucheng Xiang

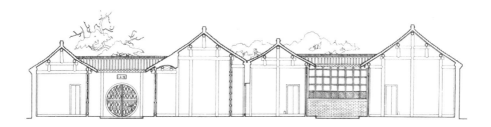

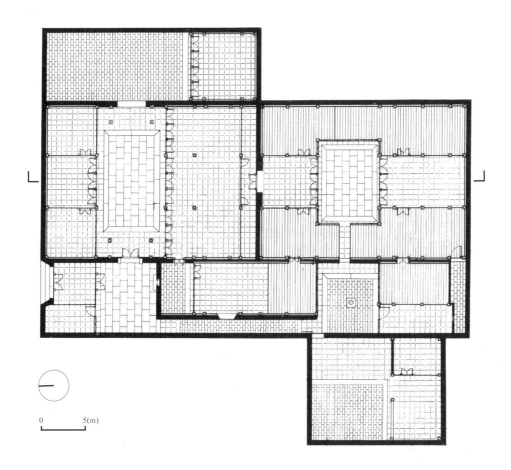

上：石牌楼林宅剖面图
下：石牌楼林宅平面图

Top: Section of Lin's residence at Shipailou
Bottom: Site plan of Lin's residence at Shipailou

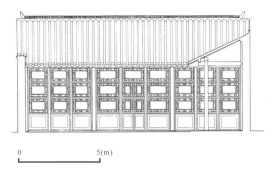

0      5(m)

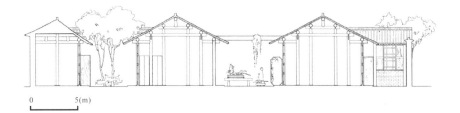

0      5(m)

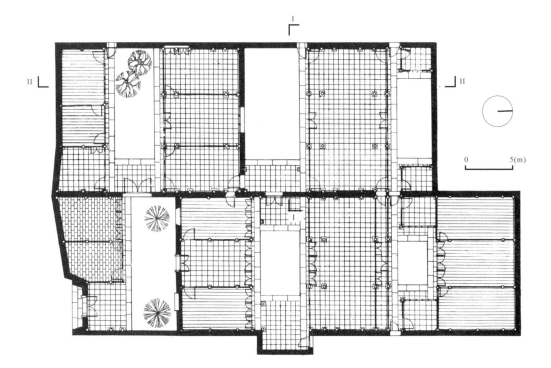

0      5(m)

上：大毛厕巷某宅 I—I 剖面图
中：大毛厕巷某宅 II—II 剖面图
下：大毛厕巷某宅平面图

Top: Section of a residence at Damaoce Xiang I-I
Middle: Section of a residence at Damaoce Xiang II-II
Bottom: Site plan of a residence at Damaoce Xiang

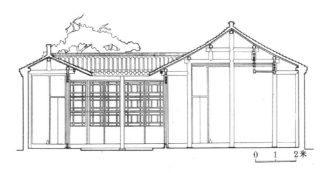

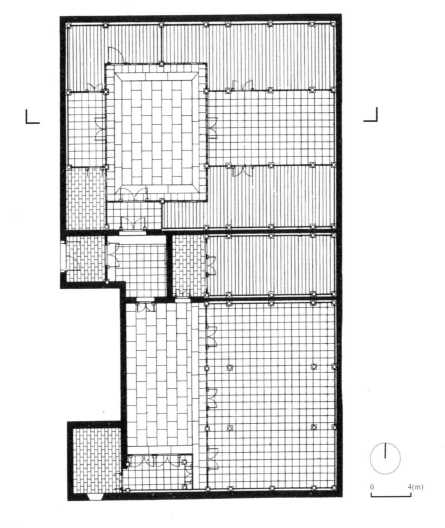

上：铰肉巷吴宅剖面图
下：铰肉巷吴宅平面图

Top: Section of Wu's residence at Jiaorou Xiang
Bottom: Site plan of Wu's residence at Jiaorou Xiang

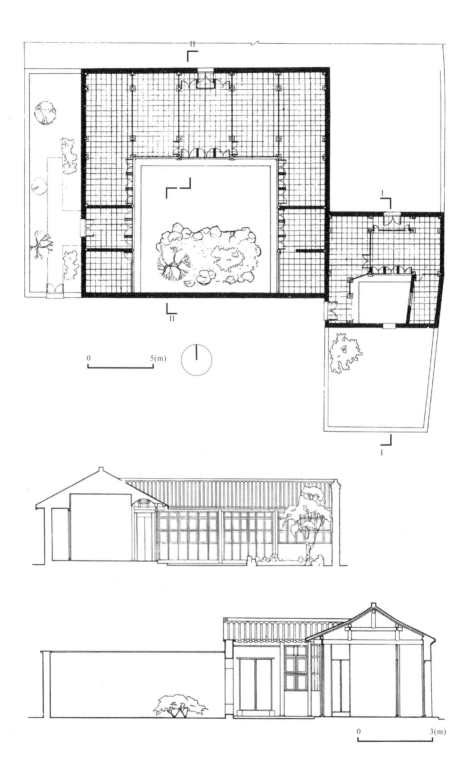

上：北柳巷七十四号某宅平面图
中：北柳巷七十四号某宅 I-I 剖面图
下：北柳巷七十四号某宅 II-II 剖面图
Top: Site plan of a residence at No.74 Beiliu Xiang
Middle: Section of a residence at No.74 Beiliu Xiang I-I
Bottom: Section of a residence at No.74 Beiliu Xiang II-II

0   5(m)

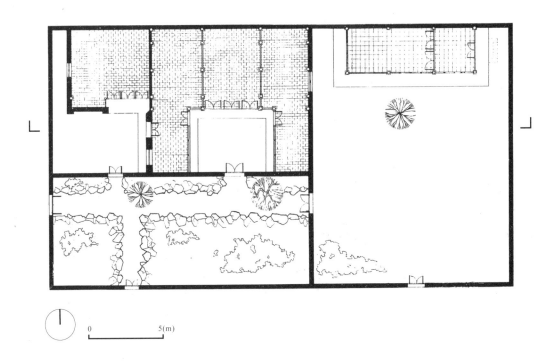

0   5(m)

上：北柳巷六十八号某宅剖面图
下：北柳巷六十八号某宅平面图

Top: Site plan of a residence at No.68 Beiliu Xiang
Bottom: Section of a residence at No.68 Beiliu Xiang

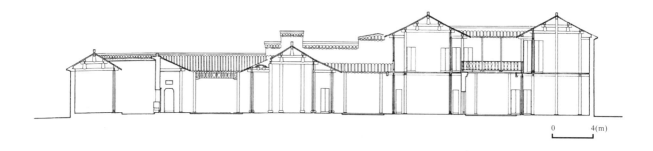

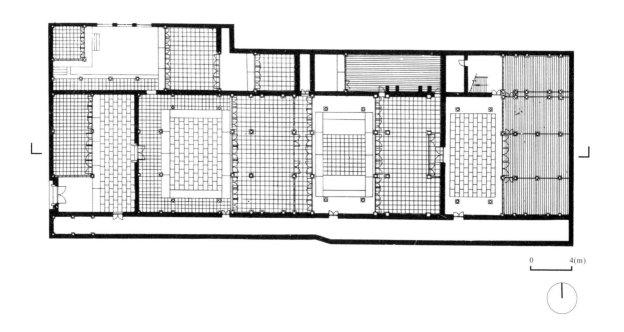

上：三元巷某宅剖面图
下：三元巷某宅平面图

Top: Section of a residence at Sanyuan Xiang
Bottom: Site plan of a residence at Sanyuan Xiang

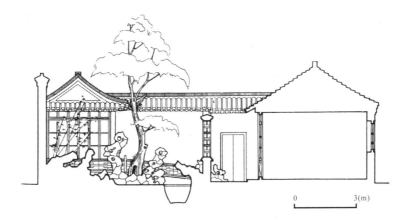

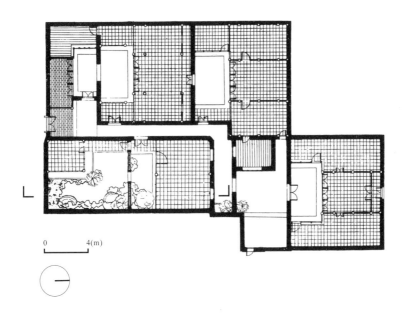

上：风箱巷杨宅剖面图
下：风箱巷杨宅平面图

Top: Section of Yang's residence at Fengxiang Xiang
Bottom: Site plan of Yang's residence at Fengxiang Xiang

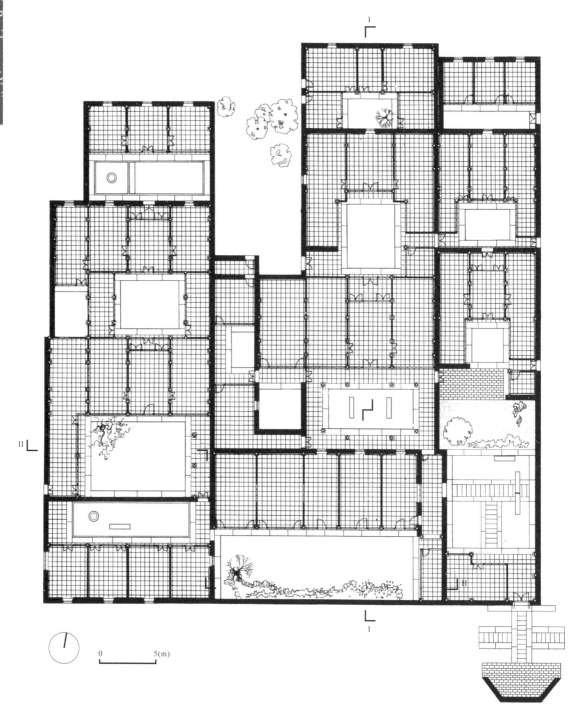

0　　　　5(m)

玉井徐宅平面图

Site plan of Xu's residence at Yujing

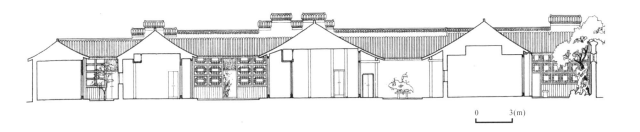

0    3(m)

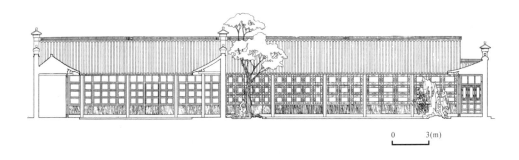

0    3(m)

上：玉井徐宅 I—I 剖面图
下：玉井徐宅 II—II 剖面图

Top: Section of Xu's residence at Yujing I-I
Bottom: Section of Xu's residence at Yujing II-II

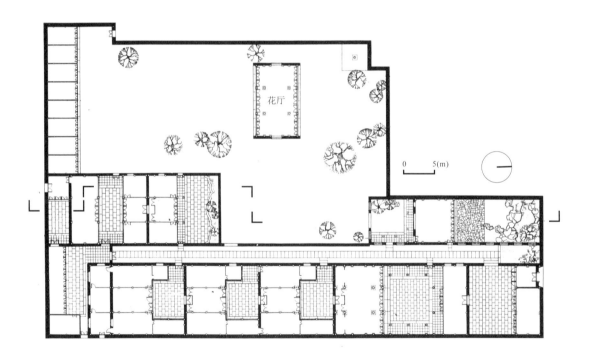

花厅

0    5(m)

上：紫气东来巷沧州别墅剖面图
下：紫气东来巷沧州别墅平面图

Top: Section of Cangzhou Villa at Ziqidonglai Xiang
Bottom: Site plan of Cangzhou Villa at Ziqidonglai Xiang

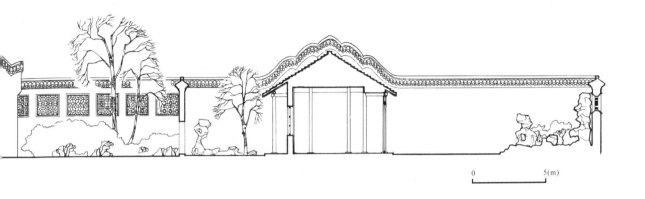

0                    5(m)

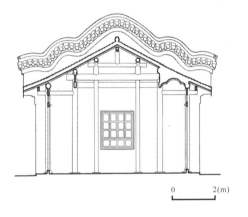

0        2(m)

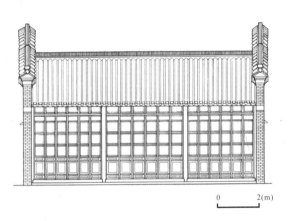

0        2(m)

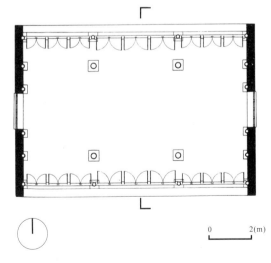

0        2(m)

中左：花厅剖面图
中右：花厅立面图
下：花厅平面图

Middle left: Section of the parlor
Middle right: Elevation of the parlor
Bottom: Plan of the parlor

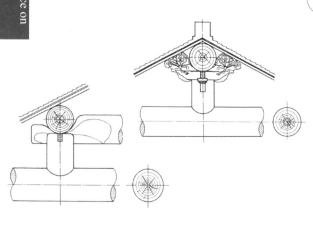

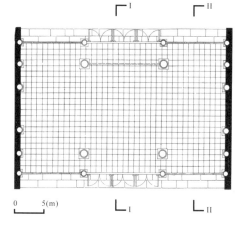

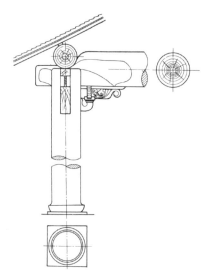

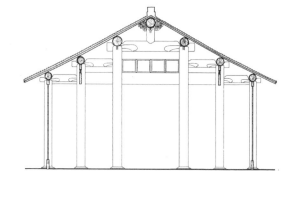

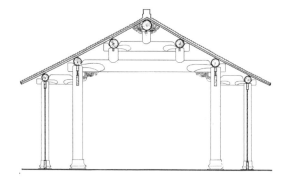

左：大东门街毛宅楠木厅木构架节点详图
右上：大东门街毛宅楠木厅平面图
右中：大东门街毛宅楠木厅 I—I 剖面图
右下：大东门街毛宅楠木厅 II—II 剖面图

Left: Detail drawing of timber frame joint, hall of *Phoebe nanmu* in
    Mao's residence on Dadongmen Street

Right top: Plan, hall of *Phoebe nanmu* in Mao's residence on
    Dadongmen Street

Right middle: Section I-I, hall of *Phoebe nanmu* in Mao's residence on
    Dadongmen Street

Right bottom: Section II-II, hall of *Phoebe nanmu* in Mao's residence on
    Dadongmen Street

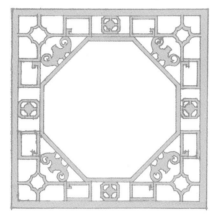

汉瓦当图

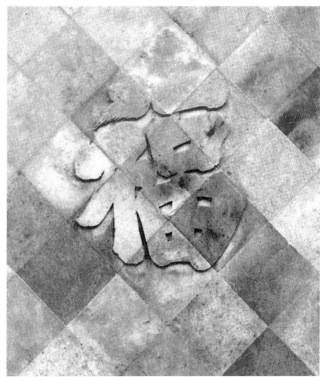

1 《水窗春呓》卷下"维扬胜地"条："扬州园林之胜，甲于天下，由于乾隆朝六次南巡，各盐商穷极物力以供宸赏，计自北门直抵平山，两岸数十里楼台相接，无一处重复，其尤妙者在虹桥迤西一转，小金山矗其南，五顶桥锁其中，而白塔一区雄伟古朴，往往夕阳返照，箫鼓灯船，如入汉宫图画，盖皆以重资广延名士为之创稿，一一布置使然也。城内之园数十，最旷逸者断推康山草堂，而尉氏之园，湖石亦最胜，闻移植时费二十余万金。其华丽缜密者为张氏观察所居，俗所谓张大麻子是也。张以一寒士，五十岁外始补通州运判，十年而拥资百万，其缺固优，凡盐商巨案皆令其承审，居间说合，取之如携，后已捐升道员分发甘肃；蒋相为两江，委其署理运司，为言官所劾，罢去，蒋亦由此降调。张之为人盖亦世俗所谓非常能员耳。余于戊戌（道光十八年，1838）赘婚于扬，曾往其园一游，未数日即毁于火，犹幸眼福之未差也。园广数十亩，中有三层楼，可瞰大江，凡赏梅、赏荷、赏桂、赏菊，皆各有专地。演剧宴会上下数级如大内式。另有套房三十余间，回环曲折，迷不知所向，金玉锦绣，四壁皆满，禽鱼尤多。……"

1. "Weiyang Shengdi"(Scenic Spots of Weiyang), *Shuichuangchunyi* (*A Daydreamer's Murmurings in Spring by a Waterside Window*): Yangzhou's gardens are the best in the whole country. On the Qianlong Emperor's six inspection tours of South China, all the merchants tried their best to entertain the emperor. Gardens built by the merchants expanded from the north gate to the Pingshan Hall. Building and lofts covered dozens of miles of land without repetition. The best of the gardens is located where the river turns west at the Hongqiao (Rainbow Bridge), with the Xiaojinshan (Small Golden Mountain) standing in the south and the Wuding (Five Pavilion) Bridge sitting in the middle. The area around the Baita (White Pagoda) is imposing for its ancient look. When the sun sets and lantern boats sail to the notes of flutes and drums, the whole scenery is like a picture of Han Dynasty's palaces. These gardens and buildings were all designed by famous designers with high commission and construction fees. There are dozens of gardens inside the city, and the most spacious and magnificent garden among all is the Kangshan Caotang (Humble Cottage in Kangshan). And the Wei's Garden has the best artificial mountain of Lake Tai stones, which costed two hundred thousand and more taels of silver for transporting and locating the stones. The most magnificent and sophisticated garden is part of the residence of a salt-transporting conroller surnamed Zhang, whose nickname is "Zhang with pockmarks." Zhang started as a poor scholar and was appointed as the Second Assistant Salt Controller of Tongzhou in his fifties and accumulated millions within ten years. His official title was so powerful that he was in charge of all the major cases involving salt merchants. Even though he was not in charge of the cases, he could still contribute his opinions if he was compensated. With the money, he later bought an official title of circuit intendant and was appointed to go to Gansu province. Jiang Xiang, viceroy of Jiangsu, Anhui and Jiangxi provinces appointed Zhang to be in charge of the Transport Monitoring Office. Later on, Zhang lost his title after being incriminated by an imperial remonstrating censor, and Jiang's title was also dropped. Zhang might have been one of those so-called "capable officers." In the year of Wuxu (1838, the 18th year of the Daoguang reign), I married into my wife's family in Yangzhou, and I visited Zhang's Garden. A few days later, the garden was destroyed by fire, so I was lucky to have visited the garden before then. The garden was laid out on a site of several dozen mu. Visitors could oversee the whole Yangtze River from a three-story building in the garden, and there were specific places for visitors to enjoy plums, lotus, sweet osmanthus and chrysanthemum. Halls for theater and banquets were in several levels just as in royal palaces. There were also over thirty suites in loops and visitors were usually lost among the rooms. Walls of all four sides were embedded with gold, jade and brocade. There were particularly plenty of fish and birds.

2. "Guangling Mingsheng"(Scenic Spots of Guangling), *Shuichuangchunyi*: Yangzhou excels with its gardens and pavilions. Though all of them are made, they reflect the craftsmen's hearts and souls. The houses and land boats covered seven to eight li at the north of the city, but none of them are similar. It would have been impossible if there were not an accumulation of material and human resources during the Qianlong reign. During the 25-year Jiaqing reign, these buildings were already going into decay. In the year of Jimao (1819, the 24th year of the Jiaqing reign) and Gengchen (1820, the 25th year of the Jiaqing reign), I visited my mother in the south. During my trip, I could still see the Large and Small Hong (Rainbow) Gardens, which were still magnificent and circuitous, and I felt as if visiting Pengdao (Island of Immortals). Fifty to sixty percent of the gardens still existed at that time. Twenty years later in the year of Wuxu (1838, the 18th year of the Daoguang reign), when I married into my wife's family in Yangzhou, land was deserted and covered with weeds. However, outside the Tianning Gate, Meihualing, East Garden, Chengyin Qingfan, Xiaoqinhuai (Small Qinhuai River), Hong Bridge, Taohua'an (Peach Flower Nunnery), Xiaojinshan, Yunshan (Cloud Mountain) Belvedere, Chiwu (Almost Reaching the Sky) Tower, Pingshan Hall were all in good shape. During the months of May, June and July, visitors came to these places to spend their summers. Painted boats sailed on the notes of flutes and drums, and visitors appreciated the sunset and got drunk under the crescent moon. Sounds of singing flew into the clouds and the fragrance of flowers surrounded people like mist. The whole scenery could still be compared to Suzhou's and Hangzhou's scenery.

*Collected Works of Gong Zizhen, Part III*: "Revisiting Yangzhou in June of Jihai (1839, the 19th year of the Daoguang reign): 'When I was with the Ministry of Rites, a guest who had visited Yangzhou asked me, "Do you know today's Yangzhou? If you have read Bao Zhao's *Wucheng Fu* (*Rhapsody on Wucheng*), you feel you have been there." I was filled with sorrow over his words...I saw the circuitous landscape of Yangzhou that expands over 30 li. Morning rain brushed the buildings. Roof tiles of the houses were shiny as fish scales. There were no broken walls nor bricks. I began to doubt the words of the guest of the Ministry of Rites...I went to visit Shugang Ridge with a visitor and the boat ride was very fast...During the trip, the boatman would point at sites at both banks and say that was the former site of some garden or the former site of some liquor shop. The boatman pointed around eight to nine places. The Yihong (Rainbow Leaning) Garden no longer exited. I had stayed at the West Garden before. The gate and horizontal board still existed. There were about eight or nine sites that could be visited, in which there were still sweet osmanthus on land and lotuses, caltrops and Gorden euryales in the waters. The northwest corner of Yangzhou had the best scenery.'" Gong visited Yangzhou very briefly so he

2　《水窗春呓》卷下"广陵名胜"条："扬州则全以园林亭榭擅重，虽皆由人工，而匠心灵构。城北七八里夹岸楼舫，无一同者，非乾隆六十年物力人才所萃未易办也。嘉庆一朝二十五年已渐颓废。余于己卯（嘉庆二十四年，1819）、庚辰（嘉庆二十五年，1820）间侍母南归，犹及见大小虹园，华丽曲折，疑游蓬岛，计全局尚存十之五六，比戊戌（道光十八年，1838）赘姻于邗，已逾二十年，荒田茂草已多，然天宁门城外之梅花岭、东园、城闉清楚、小秦淮、虹桥、桃花庵、小金山、云山阁、尺五楼、平山堂皆尚完好，五、六、七诸月游人消夏，画船箫鼓，送夕阳、醉新月、歌声遏云、花气如雾，风景尚可肩随苏杭也。……"

《龚自珍全集第三辑》："己亥（道光十九年，1839）六月重过扬州记：'居礼曹，客有过者曰：卿知今日之扬州乎？读鲍照《芜城赋》，则遇之矣。余悲其言。……扬州三十里首尾屈折高下见。晓雨沐屋，瓦鳞鳞然，无零甃断甓，心乃疑礼曹过客言不实矣。……客有请吊蜀冈者，舟甚捷……舟人时时指两岸曰：某园故址也，某家酒肆故址也。约八九处。其独倚虹园圮无存。曩所信宿之西园，门在，题榜在，尚可识，其可登临者尚八九处，阜有桂，水有芙蕖菱芡，是居扬州城外西北隅，最高秀。'"从案：龚氏匆匆过扬州，所见甚略，文虽如是，难掩荒败之景。

钱泳《履园丛话》卷二十"平山堂"条："扬州之平山堂，余于乾隆五十二年（1787）秋始到，其时九峰园、倚虹园、筱园、西园曲水、小金山、尺五楼诸处，自天宁门外起，直到淮南第一观（疑为"淮东第一观"——编者），楼台掩映，朱碧鲜新，宛入赵千里仙山楼阁。今隔三十余年，几成瓦砾场，非复旧时光景矣。"

魏源集中有记扬州园林盛衰之诗，《扬州画舫曲十三首之一》："旧日鱼龙识翠华，池边丛鹤树藏鸦；离宫卅六荒凉尽，不是僧房不见花。（凡名园皆为园丁拆卖，惟属僧管之桃花庵、小金山、平山堂三处，至今尚存）。"《江南吟》注云："平山堂行宫属园丁者，皆拆卖无存，惟僧管三处如故。"故有"岂独平山僧庵胜园隶"句。魏氏于清道光十五年（1835）买宅于扬州新城，甃石栽花，养鱼饲鹤，名曰"絜园"，其时尚在太平天国战争之前。

235

did not see much of the city. Yangzhou's decaying state could not be covered up by Gong's remarks.

"Pingshan Hall", vol.20 of *Lüyuan Conghua* by Qian Yong : I visited Pingshan Hall for the first time in Yangzhou in the autumn of 1787, the 52nd year of the Qianlong reign. At that time, Jiufeng Garden, Yihong Garden, Xiao Garden, Xiyuan Qushui (West Garden's Winding Stream), Xiaojinshan, Chiwu Tower, and some other gardens extended from outside the Tianning Gate to the Huainan Diyi Guan (may be referring to Huaidong Diyi Guan—the editors). Lofts and terraces in colors of red and green set off each other. Visitors felt as if they stepped into Zhao Qianli's paintings of towers and pavilions on a celestial mountain. Now after thirty years, this place has almost become a rubble-strewn land. The good old times have passed.

One of the "Thirteen Poems of Yangzhou Huafang Qu" in the collected works of Wei Yuan talked about the ups and downs of Yangzhou Gardens, "Fishes from the old times would remember the vernal greenery. Ravens are hidden in trees, while water birds rest by the pond. The detached palaces were all deserted. Flowers could be only seen in monks' rooms. (All the famous gardens were dismantled and sold by the gardeners and only three gardens managed by monks were kept till today: Taohua'an, Xiaojinshan and Pingshan Hall.)" In the notes to "Jiangnan Yin" (Chanting about Jiangnan), Wei remarked, "All the places in the temporary palace in Pingshan Hall were dismantled and sold by gardeners and only the three places managed by monks were kept the same." Hence, there exists a saying that "Monks in Pingshan are better than the gardeners." Wei bought a house in the New City of Yangzhou in 1835, the 15th year of the Daoguang reign, in which he piled up rocks, planted flowers, raised fish and fed crane. The garden was named Jie (Brightness) and it existed before the war started by the Taiping Heavenly Kingdom.

3 据友人王世襄说："所谓'周制'，当指周翥所制的漆器，见谢堃《金玉琐碎》。……故钱泳说'明末有周姓者，始创此法'，不可信。"

3. According to my friend Wang Shixang, "The so-called Zhou's Principles were first applied to the lacquerware made by Zhou Zhu. The evidence can be found in Xie Kun's book, *Jinyu Suosui* (*Gold and Jade in Odds and Bits*)...Hence Qian Yong's remarks regarding the origin of the Zhou's Principles cannot be trusted."

4 朱江同志据扬州博物馆藏王氏遗嘱，认为应作"王庭余"，殁于道光十年（1830），寿八十。

4. According to Zhu Jiang, Wang's testament collected in the Yangzhou Museum indicate that the name should be Wang Tingyu, who died at the age of 80 in 1830, the 10th year of the Daoguang reign.

5. From vol.5 of *Jiangdu Xian Xu Zhi* of the Jiaqing reign of the Qing Dynasty, "Pianshi Shanfang located at Huayuan Xiang was built by Wu Jialong. There was a pond and a pavilion by a

meandering stream. The pond was surrounded by Lake Tai stones on three sides, and the tallest stone was extraordinarily beautiful. Atop the stone stood a Buddhist pine, whose trunk was one armspan in girth. None of these exist today."

From vol.12 of *Jiangdu Xian Xu Zhi* of the Guangxu reign of the Qing Dynasty, "Pianshi Shanfang located at Huayuan Xiang, also known as Shuanghuai Garden, was Wu Jialong's villa. Wu Huimo from Guangdong Province was asked to renovate the garden. The garden features Lake Tai stone rockeries, whose form echoes the image of nine lions. Each lion-like stone shows exquisite craftsmanship and a vigorous and agile character."

Compiled extensively during the Guangxu reign of the Qing Dynasty, vol.5 of *Yangzhou Fu Zhi* (*The Gazetteer of Yangzhou Prefecture*), "Pianshi Shanfang is located at Huayuan Xiang on Xuningmen Street, also known as Shuanghuai Garden, and was originally owned by a Yangzhou native, Wu Jialong. The pond was embellished with Lake Tai rocks, to create an image of nine lions. The rocks portrayed the lions' vigorous and agile character. Today, Wu Huimo owns the place."

*Huajianhuayu* (*Words Among Flowers*), "Pianshi Shanlou belongs to Wu ZhiFu, who styled himself as Zhuping. The monk named Mushan placed rockeries in the garden. The garden has Tingyu (Rain Hearing) Veranda, Pinglei (Wine Bottle) Studio, Hudie (Butterfly) Hall, Mei (Plum) Tower, and a waterside pavilion. Today, only Tingyu Veranda and the waterside pavilion make up the Shuanghuai Tea Garden." The book was published rather late in 1820, the year of Gengchen in the Jiaqing reign. The author stayed in Yangzhou for a little while, so the book's information may be wrong.

6. Chen Hongshou, who styled himself as Mansheng, was one of the eight founding partners of the Xiling Seal Engravers Society. He was born in 1768, the 33th year of the Qianlong reign in Hangzhou, and died in 1822, the second year of the Daoguang reign.

7. According to my friend Geng Jianting, "The rockery was also on the pond, while snow accumulated, the rock appeared together like nine lions. The rockery has been ruined."

8. Recorded by Kong Wuzhong, cited in vol.15 of the *Nenggaizhai Man Lu* (*Random Notes of "That Can Also Be Changed" Studio*).

9. Including engravings on brick, ivory, wood, stone, bamboo, lacquerware, jade, and porcelain.

5 清嘉庆《江都县续志》卷五："片石山房在花园巷，吴家龙畔，中有池，屈曲流前为水榭，湖石三面环列，其最高者特立耸秀，一罗汉松踞其巅，几盈抱矣，今废。"
清光绪《江都县续志》卷十二："片石山房，在花园巷，一名双槐园，县人吴家龙别业，今粤人吴辉谟修葺之，园以湖石胜，石为狮九，有玲珑夭娇之概。"
续纂光绪《扬州府志》卷五："片石山房在徐宁门街花园巷，一名双槐园，旧为邑人吴家龙别业，池侧嵌太湖石，作九狮图，夭娇玲珑，具有胜概，今属吴辉谟居焉。"
《花间花语》："片石山楼为廉使吴之黼字竹屏别业，山石乃牧山僧所位置，有听雨轩、瓶棑斋、蝴蝶厅、梅楼、水榭诸景，今废，只有听雨轩、水榭为双槐茶园。"书刊于嘉庆庚辰（1820）为时较晚，作者留扬时间甚短，似出误传。

6 陈鸿寿，字曼生，杭州人，西泠八家印人之一，生于清乾隆三十三年（1768），殁于道光二年（1822）。

7 据友人耿鉴庭云："九狮石在池上亦有，积雪时九狮之状毕现，今毁。"

8 《能改斋漫录》卷十五，芍药条引孔武仲《芍药谱》

9 砖刻、牙刻、木刻、石刻、竹刻、漆刻、玉刻、瓷刻。

## 代后记 | In Lieu of Afterword

### 突然接到陈从周教授寄赠的《扬州园林》
### Suddenly Received *Yangzhou Gardens* Gifted and Mailed by Prof. Chen Congzhou

一九五六年，同济大学建筑系印行陈从周教授编撰的《苏州园林》。我汇去五块钱购得一册，随时翻看，非常喜爱。苏州园林多，大部分摄在相片里的园林我都没到过，可是最好、最著名的几个全是我幼年时经常去玩的。拙政园、沧浪亭、怡园、留园、网师园，几乎可以说每棵树、每道廊、每座假山、每个亭子我都背得出来。看了这几个园的相片，彷佛回到了幼年，遇见了旧友，所以我喜爱。相片中照的虽是旧游之地，却好像从前没有见过这一景，于此可见照相艺术的高妙，所以我喜爱。每张相片之下题着古人的词句，读了词句再来看相片，更觉得这一景确乎是美的境界，所以我喜爱。可惜的是词句之下没有标明是谁的词句，什么调。再则，相片之外还有测绘精确的各个园的平面图，各处亭台楼阁的平面图或立面图，以及窗槅、花墙之类的精细图案，这些是我国古建筑史中的珍贵资料，虽是外行也懂得，所以我喜爱。还有一点，这本图册不是陈从周教授个人的著作，是他带领建筑系的同学出外实习的产物，这样的实习是最好的教学方法，最合于教育的道理，所以我喜爱。

In 1956, Architecture Department of Tongji University printed and released *Suzhou Gardens*, written and compiled by Professor Chen Congzhou. I mailed 5 yuan for a book. I read the book a lot and liked it very much. There are many gardens in Suzhou. I haven't been to most of the gardens photographed in the book, but I have been to the most famous ones from my childhood: Zhuozheng Garden (Humble Administrator's Garden), Canglang Pavilion, Yiyuan Garden, Liuyuan Garden (Lingering Garden), Wangshi Garden (Master-of-Nets Garden). I could memorize every tree, every corridor, and every pavilion in those gardens. I like these photos because when I saw those gardens, I felt as if I were a child again, meeting old friends. The photos portrayed the places I have visited, but I feel I have never seen the places before, which is the ingenuity of photography. There were words and phrases by ancient writers under the photographs. Reading the words and phrases, and then looking at the photos again enhances the state of beauty of the places. The pity is that the words and phrases are not marked with their authors or titles. In addition to photographs, there were carefully surveyed plans and elevations of the gardens, pavilions, lofts, belvederes, and detailed drawings of balustrades, latticed windows and so on. Even people not in the architecture field can understand these precious materials from Chinese architecture history, and that is why I like the book. Moreover, this book is not only a personal work of Professor Chen Congzhou, but a result of him leading architecture students during their internship. I like it because this kind of internship is the best teaching method.

Eighteen years later, I started corresponding with Chen Congzhou through letters, and since then I found that he is good at painting. He gifted several paintings of plums, orchid, pine trees, bamboos and in December, 1974. I respectfully replied with a poem titled "Dongxiange" (the name of a tune of ci poem), which is copied here:

I have been fond of gardens for years.

Zhuozheng and other photos have summoned my memory.

In these gardens, I remembered playing with friends in childhood.

We ran over the rockery mountains, the stairways, the lofts, the corridors, and the waterside.

During our correspondence this fall, I received a fine jade by sending bricks.

The paintings vividly portrayed their subjects.

Red plums are primitive and interesting; orchids are refreshing and gorgeous,

And they are accompanied with thin bamboos and animals.

I hope that we can visit Canglang and Huqiu,

To have an elegant meeting and appreciate the exquisite gardens together.

It has been ten years since I wrote that poem, and during the ten years, we have had several meetings but we never realized our wish of visiting Canglang Pavilion and Huqiu Hill together.

Last year, *Suzhou Gardens* was printed again in Japan. Mr Zhou Yingnan acquired the book

过了十八年，我跟从周开始通信，这才知道他善于绘画。承他画了好多幅梅、兰、松、竹赠我，我在一九七四年十二月间回敬他一阕《洞仙歌》，现在抄在这儿：

园林佳辑，已多年珍玩，
拙政诸图寄深眷。
想童时常与窗侣嬉游，
踪迹遍山径楼廊汀岸。

今秋通简札，投览招琼，
妙绘频贻抱惭看。
古趣写朱梅，兰石清妍，
更风筱幽禽为伴。
盼把晤沧浪虎丘间，
践雅约兼聆造形精鉴。

到现在十年了。十年间虽然晤谈好多回，同游沧浪亭和虎丘的愿望可没有实现。

去年，《苏州园林》在日本重印了。新加坡周颖南先生从日本买了，寄一册赠与我。内容跟旧本全同，装订比旧本好。经过了将近三十年，旧本大概很难找到了，把它重印是必要的，因为它是有用的书，不是泛泛的书。

最近突然接到从周寄赠的上海科学技术出版社出版的《扬州园林》，在我可以说又惊又喜。为什么惊？因为他又编成了《扬州园林》，今年出版，一个字也没跟我提起过，却突然寄来了这样一本《苏州园林》的姐妹编。印刷、装订都挺精美，还有十几张相片彩色精印，是《苏州园林》所没有的，又怎么能不叫我喜呢？

我第一次游扬州是在二十世纪的二十年代，最初的好印象就是诗词中常用的"绿杨城郭"四个字。那么柔和茂密的葱绿的垂杨柳在春风中轻轻翻动，从来没见过，感到那是没法说清楚的美。后来又到过扬州三四次，都跟第一次同样匆匆，所以除了瘦西湖及其周围的若干必游处所，扬州的名园一个也没到过。现在有了这本《扬州园林》，我可以从从容容"卧游"了，因此越发感激从周寄赠此册的厚意。

《扬州园林》中有从周撰写的一篇概说，小字密排，两万多字。我视力极度衰退，没法看，想让孙辈念给我听，他们不得空闲，所以至今还没

from Japan and sent me one. The contents are the same as the old version, but the binding is better. It has been thirty years, so the old versions are hard to find. Reprinting the book is very important, because it is a very useful book.

Recently, I was gifted *Yangzhou Gardens* by Congzhou and the book is printed by Shanghai Scientific & Technical Publishers. I was surprised and happy at the same time. Why surprised? Because he again compiled together *Yangzhou Gardens*, and the book was published this year. He did not mention anything to me about the book. Suddenly, I received the sister book of *Suzhou Gardens*, whose printing and binding are both very exquisite. There are also a dozen color photographs in the book, which were not in *Suzhou Gardens*. How can I not be happy?

I visited Yangzhou for the first time in the 1920s, and my original good impression was symbolic of the phrase always mentioned in poems of "green willows around city walls." I have never seen such gentle and lush hanging willows ruffle in the spring breeze, which is a kind of beauty that I cannot describe. I visited Yangzhou again for three to four times, as rushed as the first visit. I have only visited the tourist attractions such as the Slender West Lake and some others, but I have never been to any other famous gardens in Yangzhou. Now with the book *Yangzhou Gardens*, I can "sleep and visit" the gardens without any rush. Therefore, I am really grateful that Congzhou sent me this book.

In *Yangzhou Gardens*, there is an introduction written by Congzhou, which has over 20 thousand words, and the texts are very small. My eyesight is extremely poor, so I was not able to read it.

I want my grandkids to read it out loud for me, but they haven't got free time, so I haven't read the introduction till now. However, I did read the five articles in *On Chinese Gardens*. I read about 10 pages every day and finished it with my perseverance. *On Chinese Gardens* is *Journal of Tongji University*'s offprint, so the words were printed large and I was able to read it. The five articles in *On Chinese Gardens* expressed all of Congzhou's thoughts on the art of gardening. His opinions on philosophy, aesthetics, and architecture were all included in the book. Today, there are projects organizing tourist attractions and renovating ancient architecture. The intention of Congzhou writing the five articles in *On Chinese Gardens* is to help the people in charge of organizing and renovating so they know how and what to fix. If they don't have the knowledge, then it is possible that good causes become bad results. Therefore, I believe that the five articles have good intentions, and are not just random thoughts. And the two books *Suzhou Gardens* and *Yangzhou Gardens* are visible examples because of the photographs. Using these two illustrated books and *On Chinese Gardens* could be used at the same time must be more beneficial for organizing and repairing ancient architecture. Therefore, I would like to suggest to those who care about fixing and repairing that if you enjoy the two illustrated books about Suzhou and Yangzhou, then please also read the five articles in *On Chinese Gardens* written by Congzhou.

I have always wanted to contribute some of my ideas to Congzhou. However, I have so many ideas and it been hard to organize them all, and that is why I haven't written them down. Now if I think about it, I have no idea till when I would be able

听见这篇概说。然而，从周的《说园》五篇却是我自己看的，每天看十来页，持之以恒，居然看完了。因为那是《同济大学学报》的抽印本，大字楷书，我还能对付着把它看清。这五篇《说园》是从周对造园艺术的全部思想的表达，他的哲学、美学、建筑学的观点全都包容在里面。如今，在全国范围内不是正在整理名胜、修复古建筑吗？他写这五篇《说园》的用意，就在使主其事的人懂行，知道为什么要整理和修复，该怎样去整理和修复，庶几不至于弄巧成拙，把好事办成坏事。因此，我以为这五篇《说园》是有心人的话，并非偶然兴到的漫笔，至于所涉及的具体例子，在《苏州园林》《扬州园林》两本图册中看得见。图册跟《说园》交相为用，彼此参看，对整理和修复必然更有益处。因此，我想向关心整理和修复的人进言，你们既然爱看苏州、扬州两本图册，请同时阅览从周的五篇《说园》。

我久已想向从周贡献些意思，因为头绪多，不容易想清楚，难以整理得有条有理，至今还没写出来。现在我想，等待完全想清楚，整理成条理，不知将在何年何月，不如把想到的随手写些出来，写错了将来再改，写乱了将来再调整，岂不是好？因此，下文就写这些不成条理的想头。

扼要总说一句其实也不难，难在分疏细说，说得明畅、透彻。姑且先扼要总说一句：我恳切盼望从周在拍摄、测绘古园林，为整理和修复古园林尽力之外，凭他的哲学、美学、建筑学的观点，为大众造园。所谓"大众"，包括各地的居民和来自国内、国外的旅游者。

我想，如苏州、扬州的那些名园，原先都是私家所有，不是为大众修造的，当然不为大众考虑；因此，那些园只宜于私家享受。大众去游览，要感到娱目赏心，得到美的享受，就未必做得到，大多只能做到"到此一游"而已。

私家造园，当然只须为私人着想。宾朋雅集，举家游赏，估计一百人大概差不多了。游人少，园小也见（显）得宽舒。在宽舒的环境里，站在适当的地点，凭审美的眼光观看，就能发见（现）这儿有佳景，那儿也有佳景。从周两本图册里的那些相片所以特别难能可贵，就在于在那些园林全归公有，其中几个名园的游人成千上万的近三十年间，竟能够像独个儿游园似

to organize all the ideas. I think it is better I just write down all the ideas that came to me. If some are wrong, then I will correct them in the future. If some are too messy, I can adjust them later. Hence, below are my thoughts without organizing.

It is not hard to summarize one sentence. What is hard is to detail the sentence and say it clearly. At the moment, I would try to tentatively summarize one sentence: I sincerely hope that in addition to photographing and surveying the ancient gardens to contribute to organizing and repairing them, he can also create gardens with his knowledge of philosophy, aesthetics, and architecture for everyone including local residents and visitors from both China and outside China.

I believe that all the famous gardens in Yangzhou and Suzhou were all private and not built for the public, so obviously the owners did not think about the public. Therefore, all those gardens were only good for private owners to enjoy. It might not be achievable that when public visitors go to the gardens, they feel pleasant, their eyes are pleased and they are able to enjoy the beauty. Most of the public could only have the experience of "have merely traveled to this place."

Built private gardens of course only have to consider the private owners. Friends and guests gathered in the garden or the whole family appreciated the garden together. The number of people involved is around 100 people. Since there were not that many visitors, even the small gardens felt spacious. The photos of the gardens in Chen's two books are especially precious because all the gardens are now public. During the recent thirty years, some famous gardens had thousand and ten thousand visitors. In the photos, Congzhou was able to photograph the gardens as if he was touring by himself without rush, discovering good scenic spots at any time and the cameras were always ready to photograph such nice images. I assume most visitors were not able to do the same. When there is a crowd, there is not even enough time to prevent crushing and taking care of ones' company, even if the visitors had aesthetics, they were probably too busy to appreciate. It is probably difficult for visitors with cameras to take photos. Firstly, while in a rush, there is no time to appreciate beauty. Secondly, even if one can prevent other visitors and find scenic spots, it is not possible to be away from other visitors. It is not critical to take good photographs. What is more important is that the visitors did not get to enjoy that gardens as they should have. Above are reasons why I don't think these famous ancient gardens are suitable for public to visit.

I would like to add a few more sentences on why famous ancient gardens are not suitable for public tourists. The pavilions, terraces, lofts, belvederes, halls, courtyards, artificial mountains, corridors, zigzag bridges are not suitable for the public crowd. There are not enough chairs and stools in the halls for the public to sit. No matter how spacious the halls are, there is such an unstoppable crowd flowing in the halls that one can hardly stay for a while. What is the meaning of touring then? The chairs and stools in the halls are all made of high quality timber, with very exquisite handicraft and most are marked with signs saying "Please don't sit." Some gardens don't have the signs, but who is allowed to sit? I always believe that the ancients made these seats with the intention of merely making the seats. They cared about the complexity of the composition and the

的，从从容容地凭他的审美观点，随处发见（现）佳景，随时对准镜头，摄成那么多的精美相片。我料想多数游人未必能够如此。在挤挤攘攘之中，预防碰撞和照顾同伴还来不及，即使有审美的素养也顾不到审美了。带了照相机的人也难办：一则在扰攘之中无从审美；二则即使能在意想中排除其他游人，发见（现）美景，实际上又怎么能排除呢？照不成好相片也无关紧要，紧要的是游园而没有得到应得的享受。以上是我以为古名园不甚适宜于大众游览的一层意思。

再就古名园不甚宜于大众游览加说几句。古名园的亭、台、楼、阁、厅堂、庭院以及假山、回廊、九曲桥之类不宜于大众的"挤"，厅堂里的那些椅子、凳子不适于也不够供大众的"坐"。无论厅堂的面积多么大，川流不息的人群在里面的"流"，不容停一停步，挤进去了就挤出来，这有什么意思？厅堂里的那些椅子、凳子全是上好木材，精工巧制，大多标明"请勿坐"，有的园不标明，但由谁去坐呢？我一向有个感觉，古人制造那些讲究坐具抱的是"为坐具而坐具"的观点，讲究的是构图的繁简，雕琢的精粗之类，坐上去身体舒泰不舒泰，那是不考虑的。说得明白些，那些讲究的坐具坐上去并不舒坦，不如现今的藤椅和沙发。

以下再说一层意思。古名园往往要求"万物皆备于我"，而"万物皆备于我"就一方面说，是挺高妙的一种思想境界；就另一方面说，却是私有欲的表现。私家园林之所以为"私家园林"，即为富绅豪商和皇帝私人所有。为了要求"万物皆备于我"，往往出现不配称的园林布局。厅堂前面或后面堆起一座假山，不怎么大的荷花池旁边来一艘旱船，就是例子。厅堂和假山，荷花池和旱船，拆开来看都不错，合起来看就见（显）得不呼应，不谐和。这对于如今的游览大众是不甚相宜的。有的人看了以为这样布局就挺美，有的人看了不免怅然，心里在摇头。这在供应大众以又适当又充分的美的享受以及逐步提高全社会的精神文明这两点上，都不免有所欠缺。

关于假山，在这儿我想说几句。现在为大众造园，只须因地制宜，不要求"万物皆备于我"，没有真山就不用堆假山。莫说堆假山的好手不容易找，假如有，在整理和修复古名园

delicacy of the carving. The did not care about whether it was comfortable or not to sit on the seats. To be clear, their seats is not as comfortable as today's wicker chair and couches.

Here is another thing. Ancient gardens usually strive for the feeling that "everything is prepared for me." On one hand, "everything is prepared for me" is a rather ingenious ideological level; on the other hand, it is the representation of private desire. This is the reason why private gardens are private, which is the same of gardens owned by rich merchants, government officials and the emperors. In order to achieve the state that "everything is prepared for me," a lot of unreasonable layouts were created. An artificial mountain is constructed in the front of the back of the hall. A land boat sits beside a medium-sized lotus pond. These are all examples. Halls and artificial mountains, lotus ponds and land boats. These are all great individual elements, but they don't appear very harmonious while put together. These layouts are not suitable for today's touring visitors. Some might find these layouts beautiful, but others might feel disappointed. The gardens not only are unable to be fully and suitably enjoyed by the public, but also are unable to improve society's spiritual development step by step.

Regarding artificial mountains, I would like to share some thoughts. Nowadays, when building gardens for the public, gardens only have to adapt to the sites. They don't have to achieve the feeling that "everything is prepared for me." If there are no real mountains, then there is no need for artificial mountains. Not to mention it is hard to find craftsmen good at piling up rockeries. Even there are good craftsmen, they can do other things such as fixing and repairing ancient gardens.

As a person outside the field, I have expressed enough ideas. I really hope that Congzhou could build public gardens. I have already two specific projects and I will write them down now. They are also words from a person outside the field.

I propose the first project of building sightseeing districts for public enjoyment under the condition of not expropriating or expropriating as little as possible the agricultural lands around the Lake Tai. The design intention is based on natural elements, with small corrections and revisions, and the goal is to benefit the public's physical and psychological conditions. If we build hotels in these districts, then we should express the vernacular architecture's characteristics. Food and service wise, everything should be designed for the touring public, to let them be fully satisfied. Never build tall buildings like fire match boxes. Those are the forced results of cities, and I have no idea what the feeling of living inside might be. I have learnt from photos or TVs. No matter one single tall building or multiple buildings, I always felt they are the ugliness of big cities. Our tourist districts around the Lake Tai must not learn from them.

Another project I propose is that based on research, we can categorize and design different typologies for all villages. First is the typologies for the houses in the villages. Second is that for the courtyards in the front and the back of the houses. Nowadays, farmers from all around have grown more and more affluent. They are looking not only for spacious houses to live in, but also for comfortable houses so they feel happy with their material and spiritual conditions. To design and make the drawings for the farmers is a great thing to do. Regarding the layout in the front and

的工作中会大有用武之地。

外行话说得不少了，应该就此打住了。我恳切盼望从周为大众造园，想到两个具体的项目，现在就写出来，其实也不可能不是外行话。

一个项目是以太湖周围为范围，在不征用或尽少征用农田的前提下，挑选若干地点，兴建游览区，供大众享受。一切利用自然而加以斟酌修正，务求有益于大众的身心。如果在游览区修建旅舍，应该显示出当地建筑的特色，而饮食起居和供应服务各方面务必专心致志为游览的大众着想，使他们心里真个满意。千万不要修建"火柴匣式"的高楼。那是大城市不得已的产物，我不知道住在里边是什么滋味。我从相片或电视中看，无论单座高楼或多座高楼，总感到这是大城市异常的"丑"。咱们太湖周围的游览区不能学它。

再一个项目是在调查、研究的基础上，分成若干类型，按类型为各地农村绘制两种设计图案，一是住房的设计图案，二是屋前、屋后园圃的设计图案，以供广大农民采用。如今，各地农民逐渐走上富裕的道路，他们不但要求有足够的房子住，还要求住得舒服，生活上、精神上更感到愉快。在这方面为农民服务，设计制图，真可谓无量功德。至于屋前、屋后的布置，经过专家的考虑，可能做到更经济、更美，也不是无关重要的细事。这个项目好像不是造园，其实是广义的造园。

以上说的两个项目，当然要由从周带领同济大学的同学们共同去做。那么，这样做是最高明的教学方法，同时又是最踏实的教育实践。

从周精力充沛，不怕多事，学力和经验两扎实，看了我提出的两个项目，想必会跃跃欲试；可惜我说得不透彻，欠具体，通篇看来，更见（显）得杂乱无章。用这样的拙作来报答从周寄赠《扬州园林》的厚意，就从周方面说，与拙词《洞仙歌》里的句子正相反背，可谓"投琼招璧"了。

叶圣陶

一九八三年七月十二日作完

the back of the houses, experts could make them more economical and beautiful, which is not an insignificant task. This project will not just build gardens but build them in a more general context.

The two projects mentioned above should be led by Congzhou, with students from Tongji University. Therefore, it will be the most ingenious education method with the most applied practices.

Congzhou is full of energy and not shy of tasks. He has sound knowledge and experience. If he sees the two projects I proposed, I am certain he will definitely want to try them. The pity is that I did not illustrate the projects with all the details. The article seems messy without organization. I use such clumsy work to pay back Congzhou's gift of *Yangzhou Gardens*. From Congzhou's side, this is the opposite of the sentence from my poem "Dongxiange," that is "sending a fine jade and receiving bricks."

Ye Shengtao

Finished on July 12th, 1983

图书在版编目（CIP）数据

扬 州 园 林 与 住 宅：纪 念 版 = Yangzhou Gardens and Traditional Residences
（Centenary Edition）：汉、英 / 陈从周著 . -- 上海：同济大学出版社，2018.11
ISBN 978-7-5608-8168-3

Ⅰ . ①扬… Ⅱ . ①陈… Ⅲ . ①古典园林－园林艺术－扬州－汉、英
Ⅳ . ① TU986.625.33

中国版本图书馆 CIP 数据核字 (2018) 第 219585 号

## 扬州园林与住宅

陈从周 著

英文翻译：乐正阳    摄影：陈从周    封面摄影原作：金宝源（《扬州园林》，1983）
书名与题字书法：乐峰

出 版 人    华春荣
责任编辑    罗璇 武蔚
责任校对    徐春莲
装帧设计    博风建筑

出版发行    同济大学出版社    http://www.tongjipress.com.cn
           地址：上海市四平路 1239 号    邮编：200092    电话：021-65985622
经    销    全国各地新华书店
印    刷    上海丽佳制版印刷有限公司
开    本    787mm×1092mm    1/16
印    张    15.5
字    数    387 000
版    次    2018 年 11 月第 1 版    2021 年 12 月第 2 次印刷
书    号    ISBN 978-7-5608-8168-3
定    价    95.00 元